State Intervention and Business in China

To our Alma Mater – Fudan University

State Intervention and Business in China

The Role of Preferential Policies

Ding Lu and Zhimin Tang

Edward Elgar
Cheltenham, UK • Lyme, US

Published by
Edward Elgar Publishing Limited
8 Lansdown Place
Cheltenham
Glos GL50 2HU
UK

Edward Elgar Publishing, Inc.
1 Pinnacle Hill Road
Lyme
NH 03768
US

A catalogue record for this book
is available from the British Library

ISBN 1 85898 476 9

Printed and bound in Great Britain by Bookcraft (Bath) Ltd

Contents

Charts

Tables

Acronyms

APEC	Asia–Pacific Economic Cooperation
BOP	balance of payment
CEO	Corporate Executive Officials
CPC	the Communist Party of China
FDI	foreign direct investment
GATT	General Agreement on Tariff and Trade
GDP	gross domestic product
GNP	gross national product
IMF	International Monetary Fund
MOFTEC	Ministry of Foreign Trade and Economic Co–operation
MNF	Multinational Firms
PBC	People's Bank of China
PRC	the People's Republic of China
Rmb	*renminbi* (Chinese currency unit, equivalent to *yuan*)
SEZ	Special Economic Zone
SOE	state-owned enterprise
SPC	State Planning Commission

TPT	Transportaion, Post and Telecommunications
TVEs	township and village enterprises
VAT	value-added tax
WTO	World Trade Organization

Exchange Rates

Average (Official) Exchange Rate of Foreign Currencies for Rmb (*Yuan*)

Year	US$ 100	100 Japanese Yen
1981	170.51	0.77
1982	189.26	0.76
1983	197.57	0.83
1984	232.70	0.98
1985	293.67	1.25
1986	345.28	2.07
1987	372.21	2.58
1988	372.21	2.91
1989	376.59	2.74
1990	478.38	3.32
1991	532.27	3.96
1992	551.49	4.36
1993	576.19	5.20
1994	861.87	8.44
1995	835.07	8.92
1996	830.00*	7.28*

* As of 30 October 1996.

Preface and acknowledgments

A salient feature of China's contemporary market environment is the significance of state intervention toward doing business in the form of "preferential policies". Anyone who seeks business opportunities in China would immediately notice these policies. The easiness getting one's business registered, the likelihood of one's investment project being approved, the availability of banking credit, and even the tax rates a firm is subject to may vary from region to region and from industry to industry. These conditions may also depend on the status of one's business partner(s). To make things more complex, the policy preferences are fast-changing and often implemented with discretion. These policies have had great influence on a wide range of economic activities, including foreign direct investment. The extent, complexity and variety of these policies are bewildering to both investors and academics who study the Chinese economy.

This book aims to provide a systematic study of China's preferential economic policies. Readers will find in this volume a transparent account of these policies and a political-economy analysis of their sources and functions. The book offers empirical observations on the policy impact of state intervention on regional development and sectoral changes. By reviewing the recent policy changes and views aired by Chinese scholars and policy-makers, this study sheds light on the prospects of China's preferential-policy system.

The book is suitable for scholars and specialists who are interested in the research on the contemporary Chinese economy and society. It can also be a useful guide for doing business in China.

The writing of this book greatly benefited from the excellent collections in the library of the East Asian Institute of the National University of Singapore (formerly the Institute of East Asian Political Economy). We are grateful to the librarians for their services.

We thank Mr Edward Elgar for offering us this opportunity to publish our work. We are very thankful to Ms Dymphna Evans, Mrs Julie Leppard, Ms Christine Boniface and Mr Jonathan Murgatroyd for their patience and professional support which have made the publication of this book possible.

Ding Lu and Zhimin Tang

Foreword

It is now almost twenty years since China began a series of economic and social reforms identified with the late Deng Xiaoping. These reforms aimed at liberalizing the economy and increasing the standard of living. Economists are divided, not equally, as to whether China's reforms are intended to secure transition to a market economy or are more limited in the intention of fully removing some significant features of the previous command-like system. Nevertheless, the reform process has produced major changes in China in terms of its openness to the outside world, its significance in international trade and its acceptance of foreign investment with the internationally accepted business practices. These changes have resulted in increased standard of living and variety of consumer goods in the country.

The two economists who wrote this book are familiar with the Chinese economy and its reform policies. They also have experience of living and working in Singapore, an economy whose economic development has been firmly based on the preferential treatment of foreign investors in the process of building up its manufacturing and financial sectors. It is therefore natural for them to turn their attention to the nature of the preferential policies China has adopted and the problems they have produced. As the authors conclude, many of these preferential policies are at a crossroads.

As the two most obvious cases of such preferential policies, the Chinese authorities created the city of Shenzhen near Hong Kong, the source of most of China's foreign investment, in 1980 and established the Pudong New Area in the reinvigorated Shanghai in 1990. Aware of the problem of regional imbalances, the authorities in recent years have nevertheless tried and had some success in attracting new investment into areas inland from the more prosperous coastal provinces. However, regional imbalances and the fate of the Special Economic Zones are just one of the issues the authorities must face. Preventing further waste of resources similar to that experienced in the early 1990s caused by uncoordinated over-investment in so-called "economic development zones" by local authorities is another challenge.

Challenges also arise from other aspects of the economy. Recently, for instance, some significant problems in the automobile industry have emerged and important projects have been cancelled or postponed. Some foreign investors have reduced their ranking of China as a destination for investment for difficulties relating to legal, tax and financing matters. Generally speaking, expected returns to capital in China for investors are relatively low if one considers the degree of risks associated with the ventures there.

As the authors point out, future reforms are likely to follow the intentions of the Ninth Five-year Plan (1996–2000) and, more importantly, the "landmark" outline of developments up to the year 2010. How these intentions, together with China's regaining Hong Kong as a Special Administrative Region and its desire to join the World Trade Organization, will change the investor climate in China and its future development are significant topics for anyone with an interest in economic development, comparative economics or business in China.

Gavin Peebles
Singapore
July 1997

1. Introduction

1.1 A TALE OF "FAKE FDI"

With her 1.2 billion population and nearly two decades of spectacular growth, China promises to become one of the world's largest economic powers and consumer markets in the next century. This potential has made her one of the most attractive host countries for foreign direct investment (FDI) in the developing world.

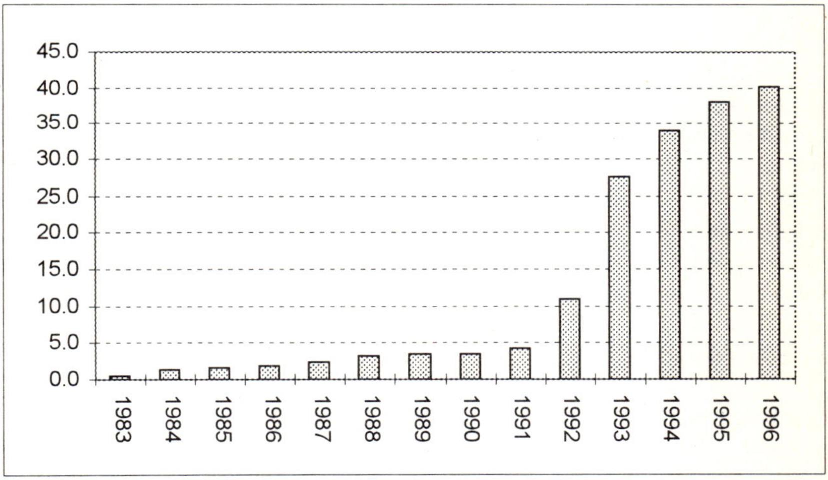

Source: State Statistics Bureau..

Chart 1.1 Actualized FDI in China, 1986–1996 (billions of US$)

The Largest Host Country of FDI in the Third World

According to the United Nations, in 1995 China accounted for more than 38 per cent of the US$ 100 billion FDI flows into developing countries. By 1995, China had ranked as the second largest host country for FDI inflows in the world after the United States for three consecutive years.[1] The latest figure from the State Statistics Bureau of China showed that the amount of actualized foreign direct investment (FDI) in China reached a record high of US$ 40 billion in 1996, a 16 per cent rise over 1995 (Chart 1.1).[2]

From 1978 to 1996, China had hosted about US$ 172 billion of FDI and had approved more than 281,300 foreign funded enterprises. By the mid-1990s, foreign-funded enterprises in China had employed 16 million people and accounted for 31 per cent of China's total exports.[3]

Foreign investors in China, however, face a rather sophisticated business environment. The sanguine figures of the FDI in China should be interpreted with caution.

All That Comes as FDI is Not Foreign

It is noteworthy that more than half of the FDI has come from Hong Kong and Macao. The proportion was nearly 70 per cent in peak years like 1987 and 1992, as shown in Chart 1.2. A considerable part of that FDI may not even be owned by business people in Hong Kong and Macao at all. This is because, among the Hong Kong firms that have actively invested in China, quite a few are subsidiaries of mainland Chinese companies.

In Hong Kong business circles, these firms are dubbed as "*zhong zi gong si*", which literally means "China-funded companies". These firms are the side products of China's interventionist policy that features unequal treatment toward investors of different types. They were set up by their domestic mother companies to take advantage of the preferential treatment only offered to foreign-funded enterprises. They transfer domestic capital into Hong Kong and then repatriate it back into the mainland in "phantom" foreign ventures.[4] Although there are no official statistics about the size of the "fake FDI" from Hong Kong, some businesspersons estimated that about 30 per cent to 40 per cent of the FDI flows into China from Hong Kong might have originated from the mainland.[5]

The Trace of "Fake FDI"

According to the balance of payments (BOP) figures published by the International Monetary Fund (IMF), there was a surge in capital outflows from China in 1992 and 1993. This can be seen in the item, "Direct Investment Abroad", which hits US$ 4.4 billion for the year 1993. This is a significant increase compared to the level of US$ 0.9 billion in 1991. The item of "Net Errors and Omission" for the year 1993 also records another extraordinary outflow of US$ 10 billion.[6] Even half of these two items added together could account for 40 per cent of Hong Kong's FDI in China for the same year.

An important clue to this mystery lies in the fluctuation in the share of the FDI flows into China from Hong Kong and Macao in China's total FDI inflow. As shown in Chart 1.2, the share of FDI from Hong Kong and Macao did follow a cyclical pattern in the period from 1984 to 1995. Its fluctuation correlates closely with the macroeconomic cycles on the mainland. The share reached two peaks in 1987 and 1992 respectively when the Chinese economy was "overheated". It plunged to two troughs around 1990 and 1994–95 when Beijing carried out its "austerity (or soft-landing) programmes" to combat runaway inflation with tight monetary policies.

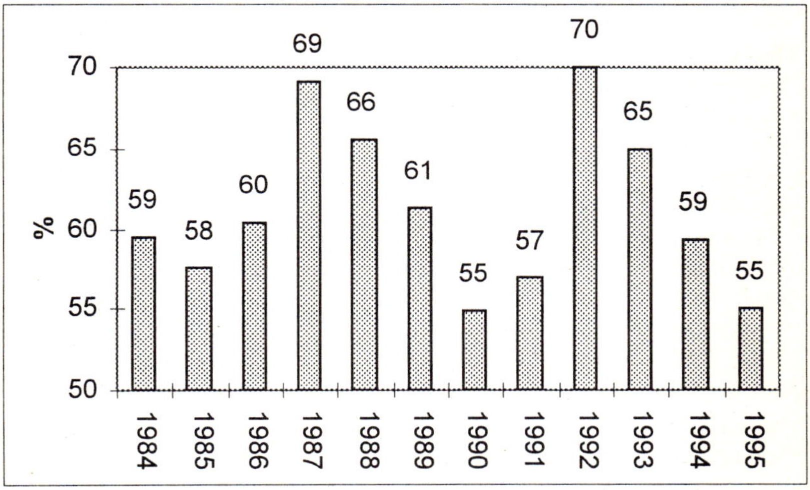

Source: *China Statistical Yearbook*, various issues.

Chart 1.2 *Share of Hong Kong and Macao's Contribution to the Actualized Annual FDI in China.*

There could be quite a few explanations why FDI from Hong Kong and Macao has behaved so sensitively to the macroeconomic fluctuations on the mainland, as compared with FDI from other countries. One possible answer is that a considerable part of the investment has come from the China–funded companies in Hong Kong. When China's domestic monetary policy was relatively loose during the overheated period, these companies would have access to more investment funds. When China's monetary policy was relatively tight during the "austerity" period, their funds to invest in the mainland would also drain away.[7]

The "round-tripping" of Chinese capital aroused serious concern in Beijing. When Beijing's *Economic Daily* raised the issue in 1988, a policy debate occurred among Chinese economists over how to deal with "phantom" foreign ventures.[8] To discourage such capital flows, the government has since taken measures to practise tighter screening and monitoring of FDI projects. By early 1994, the Chinese authorities deprived over 7,500 ventures of their status as foreign affiliates.[9] The problem of "round-tripping" investment, however, still remains.

A Wonderland of "Preferential Policies"

The tale of the "fake FDI" from Hong Kong reflects a salient future of China's contemporary market environment: the resource allocation distorted by state intervention toward doing business in the form of "preferential policies". Anyone who seeks business opportunities in China would immediately notice the existence of these policies.

How easy is it to get your business registered and licensed? How likely is your investment project to be approved? Will you be able to get loans from the banking system? What tax rates will your company be subject to?

The answer to the above questions is: "it all depends". In this wonderland of preferential policies, it depends on who you are, where you are from, and who your Chinese business partners are. It depends on which part of China your company is doing the business in and where you intend to invest. Again it depends on which industry you intend to operate in. To make things more bewildering, these policies are dynamic and fast-changing, and often implemented with discretion. Many foreign investors are confused. Some are frustrated. Quite a few, however, have been so far surfing well on these policies and making their fortunes.

1.2 BACKGROUND OF STATE INTERVENTIONISM

The term "state intervention toward business" in this book refers to government's actions and policies designed to influence firms' business decisions. State intervention discussed here involves government's role to change the microeconomic consequences of business activities. It aims to influence firms' decision on issues such as what to produce, how to produce, where to produce, and for whom to produce.

The depth and extent of China's state interventionism toward doing business are by and large a legacy of the centrally planned socialist economic system, which used to dominate economic life in China for decades. China's pre-reform economic system was initially set up in the 1950s following the model of the Stalinist Soviet economy. Although economic policy making was strongly influenced by the Maoist utopianism from the 1950s to the 1970s, China's economic system was basically a centrally planned one.

Features of the Pre-Reform Economy

The decision making over resource allocation was highly concentrated in the state. Almost all in the labour force were employed by state-owned or collective-owned enterprises and farms. The central government, through its planning agencies, set the production targets for all productive units and commanded most economic activities.

There were no market-determined prices for most goods and services. State-owned firms had little autonomy and all their profits or losses went to the state budget. The state also provided and allocated the financial and physical capital through its monobank and "production material management system".

Under the policy of "self-reliance", foreign trade was under strict state control and the economy was mainly an autarky. In short, it was not the market but the central planners who determined what to produce, how to produce, and how to distribute national products and wealth.

Major Reforms Since 1978

Since China embarked on a comprehensive market-oriented reform in 1978, fundamental changes have taken place in China's economic structure and business environment. The reform began in the rural area by dismantling the socialist collective farming and reviving household farming. Decentralization of decision making in the state sector substantially enlarged the financial responsibility and managerial autonomy at the local and enterprise levels. Along with price liberalization for consumer goods in the 1980s, the state's direct control of capital-good supply was first relaxed and later gradually gave way to the market mechanism. By 1993, planned prices only worked for 5 per cent of the industrial products (by category), down from the level of 70 per cent in 1979.[10] Meanwhile the banking system was restructured from a monobank to a central banking system with specialized commercial banks. Security exchanges have developed since the late 1980s.

Price liberalization and banking-finance reform have drastically monetarized the whole economy. Meanwhile, the proportion of government expenditure (including that of both central and local governments) to GDP has been declining over the years (Table 1.1). In the process, the banking system and financial market have replaced the state budget as the major source of business financing. For instance, state appropriation used to account for more than 70 per cent of China's total investment in fixed assets before economic reform. By 1985, the share of domestic bank loans in the sources of fixed-assets invesment rose to above 20 per cent and surpassed the share of state appropriation. By 1995, state appropriation only accounted for 3.1 per cent of the investment fund while bank loans and business fundraising each accounted for 20.97 per cent and 53.19 per cent respectively (see also Table 4.3).[11]

Table 1.1 Proportion of State Banking Deposits and Government Expenditure to GDP

	1980	1985	1990	1995
Total deposits	42.78	55.76	73.34	78.88
Government Expenditure	27.2	22.4	16.6	11.7

Notes:
(a) Figures in the first row refer to deposits in the state banking system and rural credit cooperatives.
(b) Figures in the second row refer to the expenditures of both central and local governments.

Source: China Statistical Yearbook 1996, pp. 34–36.

Parallel to domestic reforms, China abandoned the state monopoly of foreign trade business and made every endeavour to attract foreign investors. Official control of foreign currency exchange was relaxed and foreign exchange swap markets were set up in the late 1980s. The exchange rates of the Chinese currency, Rmb, were finally unified into a single market-determined rate in 1994. Beijing set up Special Economic Zones and other open zones to host FDI and offered a wide range of tax benefits to foreign investors. All these have greatly stimulated China's foreign trade businesses and encouraged the influx of foreign direct investment.

Structural Changes in the Economy

Through economic reform, China has drastically restructured its domestic economy. The state sector's share of industrial output shrank from 1978's 77.6 per cent to the current level of around 30 per cent. Meanwhile, the non-state township and village enterprises (TVEs) have increased their share of industrial output from 9.3 per cent to more than 40 per cent. Driven by the spectacular growth of the non-state sector and the coastal regions, the Chinese economy has advanced at an average annual growth rate of real GDP of over 9 per cent since 1978 (Chart 1.3). From 1978 to 1996, China's real per capita GNP almost quadrupled.

The open-door policy has transformed the Chinese economy from a near autarky to an active participant in the world economy. The share of export in GDP rose from less than 5 per cent in 1978 to more than 20 per cent in the early 1990s. By the mid-1990s, China had become the eleventh largest trading country in the world, with a total trade turnover of US$ 290 billion in 1996. China's foreign reserves at the end of 1996 stood at US$ 100 billion, the second largest in the world. The surge of foreign capital inflows since the 1980s has made China the largest Third-World host country for foreign direct investment in recent years.

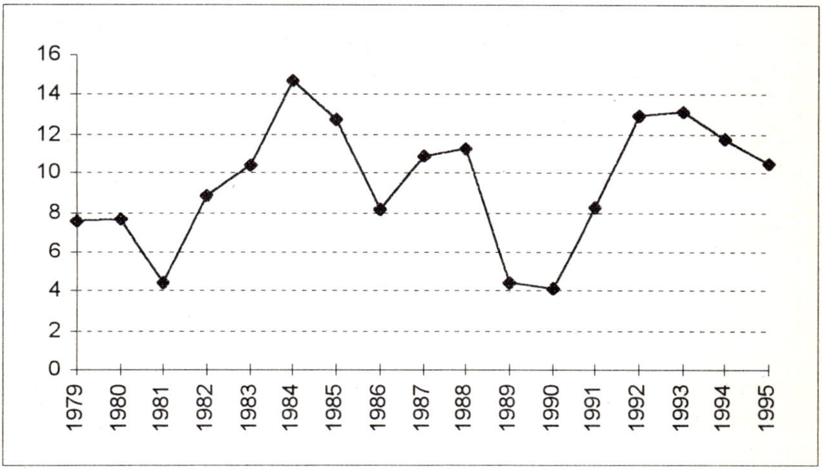

Source: *China Statistical Yearbook*, various issues.

Chart 1.3 Annual Percentage Change of Real GDP (1979–1995)

1.3 EVOLUTION OF STATE INTERVENTIONISM

Economic reform has effectively transformed China from a centrally planned economy toward a market economy. When the leadership of the Chinese Communist Party (CPC) started the process in the late 1970s, however, it did not conscientiously design the guideline for economic reform as market-oriented.

Pragmatism vs. Ideology

After years of the political turmoil of the Cultural Revolution, the most urgent task facing the Party and the government was to rescue the economy from the verge of collapse. Therefore the late Party leader Deng Xiaoping's pragmatism became the dominant principle of the Party's economic policy making.[12] This pragmatism was expressed in Deng's well-known "cat thesis" of pragmatism: "It does not matter whether cats are white or black; so long as they can catch mice, they are good cats".[13] This principle became a major vehicle for many of the reform schemes in the 1980s.

Deng's pragmatic thesis, however, remained officially within the framework of the Party's "four cardinal principles". These principles are: the socialist road (public ownership and central planning), the "people's democratic dictatorship", the sole leadership of the Communist Party, and the Marx–Lenin–Mao ideology. Therefore throughout the 1980s, it had never been on the Party's agenda of reform to transfer the Chinese economy into a full-fledged market economy in which private businesses play a dominant role.

Meanwhile the so-called "moderate reformers" consistently emphasized balanced growth under careful central planning.[14] They believed that market should play a limited, supplementary role to central planning. This view was reflected in the so-called "bird cage thesis" in the Party, which overshadowed the government's reform agenda up to 1992.[15]

From Plan to Market

Several milestones marked the evolution of China's official blueprints of reform. In June 1981, the Party's Central Committee passed "The Resolution on Certain Questions in the History of the Party Since the Founding of the People's Republic of China (PRC)". The document set the tone for economic reform: "the state economy and the collective economy are the basic forms of the Chinese economy. The working people's individual economy within certain prescribed limits is a necessary complement to the public economy. ... It is necessary to have a planned economy and at the same time give play to the supplementary, coordinating role of the market on the basis of public ownership. We must strive to promote commodity production and exchange on a socialist basis".[16]

In October 1984, the Central Committee of the CPC's "Decision on Reform of the Economic Structure" modified the official guideline by proposing to build a "planned commodity economy". The document gave the first official statement that the nature of the post-reform economy should be a "planned commodity economy" (that is, a planned market economy) and "law of value" (market demand and supply) must be consciously followed and applied. A planned economy "does not necessarily mean the predominance of mandatory planning". This "planned commodity economy" should nevertheless be based on public ownership. "Production and exchange completely subject to market coordination are confined mainly to certain farm and sideline products, small articles of daily use and labour services in the service and repair trades". All of these will "play a supplementary but indispensable role in the national economy".[17]

There was a breakthrough development in the official guideline for reform at the Thirteenth National Congress of the CPC in October 1987. The Congress's political report proposed a new thesis of a post-reform economy that resembles a regulated market economy: "the state adjusts the market, the market guides enterprises". In this "new economic mechanism", the state will "use economic, legislative, and necessary administrative means to adjust market demand and supply, to create proper economic and social environment, and to guide enterprises to make management decisions properly".[18] According to this guideline the structure of "socialist planned commodity economy" should be the one that unifies plan and market in itself.[19] The guideline also removed the restrictions on the scope of market exchange defined in the 1984 "Decision on Reform" by allowing development of factor markets of capital, labour, technology, and real estate.[20] Although the Party maintained that the main body of the ownership structure should be public, it nevertheless pledged itself to support the policy that would encourage the development of private businesses.

Crossing the River While Groping for Stepping-Stones

The evolution of the Party's guideline for reform in the 1980s reflects a carefully kept balance between ideological doctrines and pragmatic consideration of economic reality. This feature characterizes China's step-by-step and piecemeal reforms.

Throughout the 1980s there were dividing ideas within the leadership about the nature of the post-reform "planned commodity economy". As vividly suggested by the patriarch leader Deng Xiaoping, since reform is something new, the Party and the government "have to grope around to find our way like crossing the river while groping for stepping-stones planted at the bottom".[21]

This trial-and-error "strategy" has left a relatively free exploration for reform but also reflects the lack of a consistent long-term approach to reform. After the 1989 Tiananmen Square Event, the market-oriented guideline set at the Thirteenth Congress for reform was temporarily reversed in a three-year period of retrenchment and austerity programme.[22] The setback ended in early 1992 when Deng personally called on the Party to speed up reform and opening to the world.

Moving to a Full-Fledged Market Economy

On the Fourteenth National Congress of the CPC held in October 1992, the leadership reached a consensus to establish the "socialist market economic system" as the goal of the reform.[23] This agreement finally clarified the somewhat ambiguous goal of the "socialist planned commodity economy" defined at the previous national congress of 1987. In November 1993, the Third Plenary of the Fourteenth CPC Central Committee passed a 50-article "decision" on the strategies of further reforms.[24] The Party leaders announced that "establishing a socialist market economic system means making the market a fundamental factor in the allocation of resources under state macro control".[25] The "decision" covers ten broad areas dealing with the need to restructure the market system, state enterprises, government functions, taxation and social security, foreign trade and law. This document is a watershed of China's policy evolution in its transition toward a market economy.

The evolution of China's official guideline for reform has set the nature, depth, and extent of state intervention into the economy. In the backdrop to these changes in the official reform guideline, it is not difficult to understand the structure of China's preferential policies.

1.4 STRUCTURE OF PREFERENTIAL POLICIES

Preferential policies are the vehicle of government intervention. An economic policy is preferential to a business subject or economic agent if it grants the subject or agent favourable terms in receiving public services and official assistance or in fulfilling public liabilities. Under a preferential policy, the affected subject may enjoy a more supportive bureaucratic environment in getting business done. The subject may also find it easier to receive government assistance in access to economic resources. Public liabilities such as taxes and levies may be reduced or even waived for the preferred subjects. The preferential economic policies in China can be categorized into three groups, namely, the investor-oriented policies, the region-oriented policies, and the industry-oriented policies.

The Investor-Oriented Preferential Policies

There have existed many unequal treatments toward investors of different categories. On the one hand, the state-owned enterprises in general were prioritized under a soft budget constraint. Many of them received raw materials at below-market-level prices and bank loans at low or even negative real interest rates. Under the contract responsibility system, the effective tax rates for state-owned enterprises varied from enterprise to enterprise due to the manipulation of tax base and adjustment taxes. On the other hand, state-owned enterprises were subject to a heavier tax burden and were liable for miscellaneous fees and funds they had to contribute to central and local governments. Before 1994, enterprises of different ownership faced different rates of enterprise income tax. A major goal of the tax reform in 1994 was to unify the tax rates into an across-the-board 33 per cent rate for all enterprises.

For foreign investors, there have been a wide range of preferential tax treatments for foreign funded enterprises. The 1994 tax reform did not immediately remove tax perks for foreign funded enterprises located in 32 zones (including SEZs). Since then, some important preferential tax benefits for foreign funded enterprises have been phased out in the name of "national treatment".

The Region-Oriented Preferential Policies

These policies are most manifest in China's official approach toward foreign investment. The government has defined priority investment areas for foreign investors. These areas, the open economic zones, consist of three levels. In the first level are the Special Economic Zones (SEZs), which enjoy the most preferential policies. Four of the earliest SEZs, Shenzhen, Zhuhai, Shantou, and Xiamen, were set up in 1980. In 1985, the 14 open coastal cities made up the second level of open economic zones. Later in 1992, all the capital cities of inland provinces were upgraded to the second level and started to enjoy the same preferential policies as the open coastal cities. The third level covers the coastal economic areas that up to 1993 comprised 300 counties and cities. More than a dozen cities along the land border have also been opened up and belong to the third level of open zones.

More complications have developed on top of the above three-level structure in recent years. For instance, many open coastal cities have set up within their territories a number of "economic and technological development zones", which enjoy preferential policies second only to those in the SEZs. Since 1993, some provincial capitals and cities along the Yangtze River have also enjoyed some of the preferential policies of the SEZs.

The preferential policies in the open economic zones mainly include the following aspects. First, the foreign investors enjoy special enterprise income tax rates. Second, the Central Government's Ministry of Foreign Trade and Economic Co-operation (MOFTEC) has granted limited powers to local governments in approving foreign funded projects. These granted powers are not uniform across regions. Third, governments of different levels of open economic zones are delegated different latitudes of power in local economic policy making, including setting their own policies regarding foreign trade and foreign investment. Finally, there are other special treatments toward some local governments. Some coastal provinces have enjoyed special rights and privileges in foreign trade, such as reduction and waiver of tariffs, the rights to import certain commodities, etc.

The Industry-Oriented Preferential Policies

These policies reflect China's industrial policy and development strategies. China's five-year national economic plans and ten-year long-term development plans set the targets and priorities for the structural changes of the national economy. As China has been gradually transferred toward a market economy, the traditional centrally planned system has given way to a system of active industrial policies. The state uses a variety of policy instruments such as preferential tax rates, state bank loans, and trade protection or subsidies to ensure the implementation of industrial priorities.

For foreign investors, generally since the early 1980s China has had an official policy to encourage investment in manufacturing with hi-tech features and investment in infrastructure development, such as transportation, telecommunication, and energy resources. Export-oriented projects and import-substitution projects are also preferred. The MOFTEC has published lists of investment areas that are actively encouraged. Favourable approval procedures, tax concessions, cooperation from the state-owned enterprises, and other incentives are provided at central and local levels to support those preferred investments.

Plan of the Book

This book is a study of China's state intervention toward business in the form of preferential policies. The main parts of the book consist of three chapters, each of which deals with one category of these policies, namely the investor-oriented policies (Chapter 2), the region-oriented policies (Chapter 3), and the industry-oriented policies (Chapter 4).

The fifth chapter presents an analysis of administrative uncertainties in the working of these preferential policies. The last chapter highlights the trends of policy changes and discusses the prospects of China's state interventionist development strategy.

NOTES

1. United Nations: *World Investment Report 1996*, New York 1996.
2. *China Daily*, Beijing, 27 December 1996; *China Economic Information*, Beijing, 28 December 1996.
3. *Guoji Jing Mao Xiaoxi* [International Trade News], Beijing, 26 January and 6 February 1996, p. 1. *China Daily*, Beijing, 2 January 1997.
4. It is also interesting to note that China has made it clear that Hong Kong investment in the mainland would still be treated as foreign investment in terms of preferential tax policies even after 1997 when Hong Kong reverts to China. *Guoji Jing Mao Xiaoxi* [International Trade News], Beijing, 11 March 1996.
5. According to the author's interview with CEOs in one of the largest China-funded companies in Hong Kong.
6. IMF, *International Financial Statistics*, March 1996, Washington DC: IMF, p. 168.
7. On top of that, since 1994 Beijing's efforts to phase out some preferential tax benefits to foreign investors has contributed to the declining proportion of Hong Kong–Macao investment. See Chapter 2 for more details.
8. Lin , J. (1994).
9. *China Economic News*, Beijing, 16 May 1994.
10. The 5-per cent products (by category) under price control could nevertheless have been crucial to the whole economy as they covered important raw materials, energy supplies, and transportation services. By accounting value, these products accounted for approximately 20 per cent of all industrial products.
11. Statistic figures in this book, unless otherwise noted, are from the State Statistics Bureau of the PRC, *China Statistical Yearbook*, various issues.
12. Deng Xiaoping (1904–1997), Chinese Communist leader. A long-time revolutionary and Red Army veteran, Deng was the CPC's general secretary from 1956 to 1967. He was well known for being twice purged from power (1967, 1976) and twice rehabilitated (1973, 1977). Deng became the CPC's paramount leader in 1979 and served as head of the party's military commission till he retired in 1990. In his last years, Deng remained influential on the making of major policies by his hand-picked successors.
13. *Hongqi* [Red Flag], No. 16 , 23 November 1967, pp. 18–29.
14. See Harding, H. (1987), pp. 11–20 and pp. 78–83 for a more detailed description of the differences between the radical reformers and the moderate reformers.
15. The "bird cage thesis" refers to an analogy made by Chen Yun, a senior Communist leader, for his guideline of economic reform: "The economy is like a bird, and the plan a cage; if the cage is too small, the bird will die; but if there is no cage at all, the bird will fly away, unconstrained" (*Renmin Ribao* [People's Daily], 3 December 1982).
16. Liu and Wu (eds) (1986), appendix, p. 630. The term "individual economy" refers to the small-sized private firms and the term "commodity production and exchange" refers to market-coordinated production and commercial activities.
17. The Central Committee of the CPC, "Decision of the Central Committee of the CPC on Reform of the Economic Structure", in *Xuexi Cailiao* [Documents for Study], Shanghai: Jiefang Ribao Press, October 1984, pp. 2–23.
18. Zhao Ziyang, "The Report on the Thirteenth National Congress of the CPC", *Renmin Ribao* [People's Daily], 4 November 1987, p. 2.
19. Ibid. p. 2.
20. The 1984 "Decision" stipulated: "Under our socialist conditions, neither labor power nor land, mines, banks, railways and all other state-owned enterprises and resources are commodities" (Liu and Wu (eds) (1986) appendix, p. 682).
21. Xinhua News Agency, 14 September 1986, in *Foreign Broadcasting Information Service*, 16 September 1986, pp. B 1–3.

22. Premier Li Peng, in his report at the National People's Congress in April 1990, re-affirmed the necessity of mandatory central planning concerning "the production and transaction of those important products that are related to the national economy and people's livelihood". "[L]arge and medium-sized state owned enterprises should be subject to state mandatory plans or guiding plans, collective economy to guiding plans or market coordination, and individual, private, and foreign enterprises to market coordination" (Li Peng, "Report on the Third Meeting of the Seventh National People's Congress", *Renmin Ribao* [People's Daily], 6 April 1990, p. 2).
23. *Zhongguo Gongchandang Di Shisici Quanguo Daibiao Dahui Wenjian Huibian* [Documents of the Fourteenth National Congress of the CPC], Shanghai: Jiefang Ribao Press, 1992.
24. *Renmin Ribao* [People's Daily], 17 November 1993.
25. Ibid.

2. Investor-Oriented Policies

2.1 ALL FIRMS ARE NOT CREATED EQUAL

Origin Of Unequal Status

China's policy makers have a tradition of treating enterprises of different ownership-types unequally. This tradition can be traced back to the early 1950s when the newly founded Communist government endeavoured to transform all indigenous capitalist enterprises into socialist state-owned enterprises.

Unlike their Soviet counterparts, the Chinese communists did not nationalize the entire domestic capitalist economy immediately after they came to power. Instead, they designed a step-by-step procedure to "utilize, restrict, and transform" the capitalist firms. Utilization of the capitalist firms was instrumental in rehabilitating the national economy after the civil war while transformation of them into socialist state-owned enterprises was then an ideological must. Before the completion of this process of "Socialist Transformation" in 1959, there was a period when the capitalist sector coexisted with the centrally planned state sector. The official policy was to apply pressure and guidance to force the capitalist enterprises, private handicraft workers and peddlers to transform themselves from private firms to collectively owned firms and eventually socialist state-owned enterprises. Therefore it was crucial to provide preferential treatment for firms with "socialist ownership". This preferential treatment included tax benefits, bank loans, raw material supply through the state-owned wholesale sector, and government contracts.[1]

State-Owned Enterprises in Transition

Before China embarked on the market-oriented reform in the late 1970s, the state-owned enterprises accounted for about 80 per cent of the gross industrial output. The state also had a tight control over the collectively owned enterprises and rural collectives. There was very limited autonomy at the enterprise level.

In the early 1980s the basic idea of China's economic reform concerning the state-owned sector involved the separation of ownership and management.[2] This meant the delegation of decision-making power to business managers without abolishing state ownership of the means of production. The aim was to invigorate the state-owned enterprises without changing their socialist nature.

During the 1980s, the autonomy of the state-owned industrial enterprises greatly increased, especially after the Party recognized in its *Decision on Reform* in 1984 that the key to reform was invigorating enterprises.[3] Two major reform schemes were introduced in 1983 and 1984. One was the so-called "*li gai shui*" (taxes-for-profits), which sought to dismantle the system where all profits after subtracting a small retained portion for the enterprise were simply returned to the state. The reform aimed to adopt a corporate tax that would allow substantial retained earnings. By 1986, almost all enterprise profits were taxed, instead of being remitted to the government. Another was the so-called "*bo gai dai*" (loans-for-grants), which strove to move away from the provision of investment funds on a grant basis from the government budget toward the allocation of working capital and investment funds through the banking system.[4]

In 1984, the central government announced a series of measures to enlarge state enterprises' autonomy. Different forms of "management contracts" or "contracted managerial responsibility" systems[5] were applied to most state-owned enterprises.[6] According to the State Council, 90 per cent of the industrial and commercial enterprises were covered by the contracted managerial responsibility system by 1988.[7] Although these reforms did not totally overcome many drawbacks of the old system with respect to bureaucratic involvement in enterprise decision making, they greatly changed the operational environment of the state enterprises. With the reforms, the government had hardened enterprise budget constraints and made enterprise behaviour more market-oriented.

Non-State Sector under the Two-Track Approach

China's reform strategy in the early 1980s involved a "two-track approach": continued state control of state enterprises while permitting growth of a new non-state sector largely outside state control. The approach also was accompanied by the so-called two-track pricing system (or dual pricing system) in the 1980s, under which the supply prices within the state-planned sector coexisted with the free market prices.

The free growth outside the control of the state, however, would inevitably meet the limits of the established laws, rules and regulations. There also have existed many grey areas between the "two tracks", in which the authorities of control were not clearly defined. The process of reform, especially in the early stages, was characterized by a mixture of official elites' initiative and grassroots entrepreneurs' spontaneous action to break institutional barriers.

In the rural area, with the return of household farming, entrepreneurial peasants started using their newly gained freedom to set up and develop non-agricultural businesses at the township and village levels. As rural reform proceeded well by the early 1980s, Beijing also perceived the development of rural enterprises as a pragmatic and convenient solution to the unemployment problem of redundant agricultural labour. Starting in 1981, the government granted a three-year tax holiday as incentive to all new rural enterprises.[8] The rural township and village enterprises (TVEs) soon expanded their businesses to the areas that were formerly forbidden for non-state sectors. Official acknowledgment of the legitimacy of these activities came around 1983–84 through a series of policy adjustments. In 1984 the State Council issued a landmark document, which announced TVE development a national policy.[9] The new policy granted TVEs the status of "legal persons", which would enable them to obtain bank loans from state banks.

The 1980s also witnessed an overall revival and surge of the private businesses in China. Private business activities were first tolerated and later legalized and encouraged for their role of creating jobs and supplying goods and services in shortage. An amendment to the Constitution in 1988 finally led to the legalization of all private business entities, including proprietorships, partnerships and corporations.

Another fast-growing area of the non-state sector was the foreign funded businesses. With the beginning of economic reform, the Maoist self-sufficiency policy gave way to a policy of opening to the world. Beijing perceived attracting foreign investment as a key strategy in its modernization programme. To attract foreign investors, China has developed many preferential policies toward foreign funded enterprises over the years. There are also policies that specially appeal to overseas Chinese business people.

2.2 PRIVILEGES VS. EXCESS BURDENS

Unequal Tax Burdens

The "two-track approach" of China's reform inevitably led to unequal treatment toward firms of different ownership-types. After the taxes-for-profits and loans-for-grants reforms, the government still had to rely on the state-owned enterprises as its major revenue source. Apart from bearing a heavier tax burden, the state-owned enterprises also had to contribute to central and local governments' miscellaneous levies and fees. The national policy to develop rural TVEs and to attract foreign investment justified lower tax rates for the collectively owned enterprises and foreign funded ones. Therefore, before the 1994 tax reform, China had a unique corporate income tax structure that treated enterprises of different ownership-types unequally (Table 2.1).

Table 2.1 Corporate Income Tax Rates in China Before 1994

Type of Enterprises	Corporate Income Tax Rate	Other Income-Related Taxes
Large and medium-sized SOEs	55 per cent	Adjustment taxes set by local taxation authorities
Small SOEs and the collectively owned enterprises	10–55 per cent according to an 8-level progressive schedule	Other local levies on income may apply
Private enterprises	35 per cent	Individual income adjustment tax of 20 per cent on dividends and interest income may apply
Individual businesses	7–60 per cent according to a 10-level progressive schedule	Individual income adjustment tax and other local levies may apply
Foreign-funded enterprises	30 per cent (with concessionary rate of 15–24 per cent)	An additional 3 per cent local supplementary tax
Enterprises in Special Economic Zones	15 per cent	

Notes:
1. "Corporate income" refers to the firm's total profit.
2. "Individual businesses" refer to privately owned firms with fewer than eight employees.
3. "Private enterprises" refer to privately owned firms with at least eight employees.

Source: Xu and Yu eds (1994).

The heavier corporate income tax burden for state-owned enterprises, however, is accompanied by the privilege of "soft budget constraint" for these enterprises. The state-owned enterprises, especially the large and medium-sized ones, have had priority in receiving raw materials at below-market prices and state bank loans at low interest rates.

Profits in the Dual Pricing System

China introduced the "two-track pricing (dual pricing) system" in the early 1980s when the government partially legitimized the non-planned trade of raw materials, machinery, and products in the domestic market. Under the dual pricing system, official pricing of some important goods was maintained for planned supply quotas. State-owned enterprises were allowed to sell goods at prices determined by demand and supply after they had met planned supply quotas.[10]

The positive effect of the system was that the state-owned enterprises would be more market-oriented in production as their marginal products were sold at market prices. The system, however, had also become "a hotbed of economic disorder and corruption".[11] For those state-owned enterprises that had access to planned supply quotas, the gap between the official price and the market price generated lucrative businesses. The so-called "*guan dao*" (bureaucratic involvement in illegal trade) committed by official organizations became a serious social problem and obstacle to anti-corruption campaigns. Aware of this, Beijing has gradually phased out the two-track pricing system in recent years.

Bank Loans: Subsidies in Disguise

Since the loans-for-grants reform in the early 1980s, the major source of state-owned enterprises' capital financing has been the state banks. Under the current central banking structure, management of financial operation has been decentralized to local bank branches. However, the central bank, the People's Bank of China (PBC), has maintained a mandatory monetary policy through its intervention in the use of bank assets. The PBC imposes an overall credit ceiling on financial institutions as the major intermediate objective. Accordingly, the national credit planning and credit-quota allocation work together with the control of interest rates to ensure the fulfilment of the credit ceiling goal.[12]

As shown in Chart 2.1, the deposit rate and the loan rate have been almost equal to each other over the years. In some years, the loan rate was even below the deposit rate. Meanwhile, in several years when inflation accelerated, the real interest rate even became negative. From this, one can conclude that the role of interest rates has been supplementary to direct credit controls and bank credits have been near-free funds or subsidies in disguise to the borrowing firms. Accordingly, the usage of credit quotas is largely centrally planned. The state specialized banks are obliged to provide the so-called "policy loans" to meet the priorities set by the government. By 1994, such policy loans accounted for 40 per cent of the loans lent by the four major specialized banks.[13]

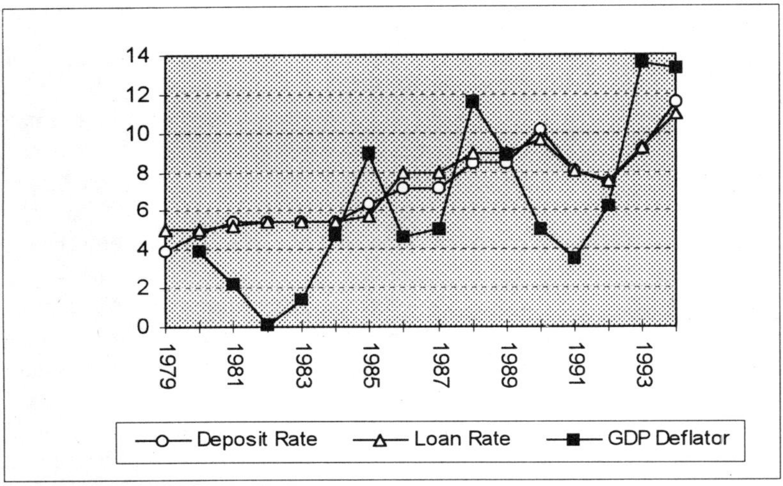

Note: Deposit rate refers to average one-year deposit rate. Loan rate refers to the average loan rate for industrial and commercial firms' circular-fund needs.

Source: *Almanac of China's Finance and Banking*, 1995.

Chart 2.1 Bank Rates vs. Inflation

Privileged access to easy and low-cost credit encourages state-owned enterprises to aggressively expand borrowing from banks, with little concern for interest costs and investment risks. Despite the fact that their contribution to total industrial output declined from 78 per cent in 1978 to 43 per cent in 1993, state-enterprise borrowing still accounted for over 80 per cent of total bank credits by 1994. According to an official survey, the average debt–asset ratio of the state-owned enterprises increased from 18.7 per cent in 1980 to 54.8 per cent in 1989 and 83.33 per cent in 1994. As a majority of state enterprises have become nil-profit earners and loss-makers in recent years, a large number of bank loans are bad loans or problematic loans in risk of default. In 1995, for instance, the nominal average capital rate of return in the state-owned enterprises was about 6 to 7 per cent, well below the 12 per cent average interest rate for business loans. By the end of 1995, bad loans accounted for nearly 40 per cent of the four specialized state banks' outstanding loans. Nevertheless, the governmental authorities insist on pumping bank loans into the state-owned sector for fear of touching off social chaos by allowing a widespread shutdown of state enterprises and a consequent massive layoffs. As a consequence, the loan volume was pulled up by the increasing losses of the ailing state-owned sector during economic slowdowns in 1981, 1986, 1990, and 1994.[14] By 1995, the debts of the 148,000 state-owned enterprises hit an appalling level of Rmb 3,360 billion (approximately US$ 405 billion), outstripping the recorded private bank deposits of Rmb 2,970 billion. Around one third of the 14,000 large and medium-sized state enterprises were in red. The Rmb 110 billion profits that healthy firms in the state sector made were virtually wiped out by the Rmb 100 billion paid in welfare costs to the state sector.[15]

"Soft Taxation"

When the tax-for-profit reform was introduced in 1983, it was expected that the relationship of state-owned enterprises to the state would be reduced to the simple submission of taxes. The enterprises would thence behave more like private firms characterized by financial independence and hard budget constraints. In the Chinese economy of the 1980s, however, market distortions were numerous and the price system continued to produce incorrect signals. The distorted profits under a uniform tax rate would leave many actually efficient enterprises suffering business losses and would encourage production expansion in the wrong sectors. The government therefore introduced an array of "corrective taxes" to compensate for profit distortions that resulted from the distorted price system and other factors that lay beyond the control of business management. In China, the factors that are beyond the control of management are called "objective conditions", while the factors of which the management is responsible are labelled "subjective conditions".

This consideration was especially important for local governments. Since these "objective conditions" existed, it was quite possible that some enterprises crucial to the local economy might not make a profit. Therefore, in the local government's view, it was necessary to subsidize these enterprises to support local economic development. Consequently, the redistribution of local business income in favour of these enterprises became an important function of local government. One way to accomplish this was to manipulate the effective tax rates of the enterprises. Although the statutory tax rates were set by the central government, the local authorities were able to set the effective tax rates by deciding each enterprise's tax base during contract negotiations. Since effective tax rates were tailored to the profit of each enterprise, the determination of the direction and the amount of compensation remained an arbitrary process of negotiation between bureaucrats and managers.[16] Even after the 1994 tax reform abandoned the adjustment taxes set by local authorities, governments of various levels may still allow arrears on payment due to government to accumulate or waive the interest payment on arrears for state-owned enterprises. According to the Ninth Five-Year Plan, an official policy to rescue the debt-ridden state-owned enterprises was to merge them with more efficient enterprises while waiving interest charges on their debts and extending the payment deadline of the principal.[17] Arrears of state-owned enterprises in industrial and commercial tax payment were up more than 70 per cent in 1996.[18]

Promotion of Local Interests

In addition to this "soft taxation" scheme, local government possessed other means to redistribute business incomes. One was charge to administrative levies on the retained profits of enterprises in the name of "concentration of funds" by local industrial bureaus or other administrative organs. The other was using their influence in banks' credit issuance. In the post-reform decentralized decision-making structure, it is in local governments' interests to compete for a larger share of bank credits since most local investment projects are no longer funded by the state's budgetary grants. In the race for bank credits, local governments try to outperform each other so as to be capable of promoting regional development and enlarging the local revenue bases. Local branch banks, on the other hand, are usually willing to cooperate with the local governmental authorities. This is because there exists a symbiotic relationship between the local governments and the local bank branches. The hierarchical administration of China's state banks parallels that of the government. The banks' executives at high and intermediate levels are appointed as governmental officials. Although local bank governors are officially appointed by the central bank, the latter must consult the local governments before such appointments.[19] The local governments, accordingly, often have a determinant role in personnel management for regional bank executives. Consequently, regional bank branches are just like semi-independent local government banks, which conduct regular banking businesses more or less beyond the direct supervision of headquarters. In such a context, there are many ways for the local authorities to push for more credits from the banking system.

Before the PBC works out the national credit plan and credit quota allocation, the localities may exaggerate their fund needs since banks' fund uses are aggregated from regional branches. After the credit quotas are allocated, local authorities may obtain extra credits from local bank branches through exerting political pressures on the latter. They may also divert bank credits from the uses originally earmarked by the PBC for certain uses to the projects that could generate quick revenues for the local government. In the process, funding for agricultural product purchase, poverty alleviation, and education development is often circumvented.[20] Since bank loans are "free" or nearly free goods in disguise, local authorities would employ all kinds of administrative measures to restrict outflow of bank funds and zealously seek cheap credits. Thanks to the symbiotic relationship between the branch banks and the local government authorities, these banks would hardly decline aggressive credit requests from the latter.

Toward Fair Play

China carried out a comprehensive tax reform in 1994. The overall goal of the reforms was to codify the fiscal rights and responsibilities of governments, enterprises, and individuals and create a fair and equitable system of taxation based on standard international practices.[21]

All firms now should have the unified corporate income tax rate of 33 per cent. There are only two exceptions. For indigenous enterprises with annual taxable profits higher than Rmb 30,000 but lower than Rmb 100,000, the income tax rate is 27 per cent. For enterprises with annual taxable profit lower than 30 thousand, the rate is 18 per cent.[22] The standard value-added tax rate, 17 per cent, applies to most items, although the rate for certain necessity items is 13 per cent. In a bid to reduce the local incentives to protect local markets, the reform also aimed to build within five years a three-tiered federalized system of taxation similar to that in the US.

2.3 "NATIONAL TREATMENT": TO BE OR NOT TO BE

During the 1980s, China offered extensive preferential tax benefits to foreign investors. These included preferential tax rates (Table 2.1) and exemption of import duty and value-added taxes (VATs) on machinery, parts, raw materials, office equipment, and vehicles (Table A1.1).

National Treatment and International Practice

Since 1994, however, Beijing has taken steps to reduce the range of these tax benefits for foreign investors. One of the motives for the policy change could be aiming at the "fake FDI" problem discussed in Chapter 1. Another motive is China's bid to join the World Trade Organization.

For policies toward foreign investment, the new buzzwords in Beijing nowadays are "national treatment" and "international practice". "National treatment" means equal treatment for foreign investors and domestic investors. There are two sides of the coin. On the one hand, foreign investors may expect fewer restrictions in doing business in China. On the other hand, they would gradually lose some of the preferential policies they have so far enjoyed.

Following "international practice" implies that China would conduct its administration of economic activities in a way similar to those in other market economies. In areas like the average tariff rate, degree of foreign exchange control, and market openness, China will apply the same standards practised in most other developing countries. Beijing has vowed to focus its future efforts to attract foreign investment more on providing a better investment environment in line with the "international practice" rather than on offering tax concessions.

Import: No Longer Tax Free

There have been so far few changes in preferential policies in the area of corporate income tax both in terms of preferential rates and tax holidays.[23] Most changes have taken place in the areas of Customs duties and VAT on imported goods (see Table A1.1). Exemptions of customs duties and VATs on imported goods in the following categories have been removed:

- Import of vehicles and office equipment by foreign-funded enterprises and open zones;
- Import of machinery[24] using the "total investment" fund by foreign-funded enterprises;
- Import of machinery and materials for construction and production by open zones;
- Import of commodities to be sold within the SEZs, or goods from barter trade in border open cities;
- Import of equipment, and materials for technological renovation or export-oriented agriculture in open zones.

Contemplating the Effects

The most important change for foreign investors in 1996 was the termination of tax exemption for the import of machinery and equipment using the "total investment" fund. Confusion in evaluating its effects often arises from the definition of the "total investment fund" of foreign-funded enterprises.

There are three different concepts related to the amount of investment in a foreign-funded enterprise in the Chinese practice: "registered capital" (*zhuce ziben*), "paid-up capital" (*shijiao ziben*) and "total investment" (*touzi zong-e*).[25] The first two concepts are clear. For any equity joint venture or a wholly foreign-owned enterprise, the investors or investment-partners must specify the size of their pledged capital when they register the enterprise. They must pay up the amount of registered capital using their own fund or other assets (e.g. machinery, intellectual property or land use rights, etc.). The paid-up capital might be less than the registered capital in the initial stage after the birth of an enterprise because the investors might choose to pay up their registered capital by several instalments.

The term "total investment", however, is a Chinese invention. It is defined as the registered capital plus the planned amount of bank loans borrowed by the enterprise of concern. The concept is a legacy of the old centrally planned system. In such a system, the material balance of the national plan must take into consideration all resources consumed (both the firm's own capital and bank loans) in an investment project. Under the stipulation by the State Administration for Industry and Commerce in China, the registered capital must reach a certain ratio of the "total investment" for equity joint ventures of different sizes. More specifically, for an equity joint venture with the "total investment" of less than US$ 3 million, the registered capital should be at least 70 per cent of the "total investment". The ratio is 50 per cent for "total investment" with the amount between US$ 3 million to US$ 10 million. For amounts between US$ 10 million to US$ 30 million, the required ratio is 40 per cent. For projects with "total investment" above US$ 30 million, the ratio is one third.[26]

Since the bank loans could account for quite a large share of the "total investment" in most foreign-funded enterprises, it makes a big difference to which level the tax exemption is applicable. Imports of machinery could be counted as part of the registered capital pledged by the foreign partner. Alternatively, they could be part of the registered capital pledged by both domestic and foreign partners. They could also be financed by the "total investment" fund, that is, the sum of the registered capital and the planned bank loans. The greater the sources of investment involved, the bigger will be the benefits brought by the exemptions of import tax.

Two Layers of Tax Exemption on Imports

A careful study of the previous Chinese Customs measures reveals that there were actually two layers of tax exemptions on the import of machinery by foreign-funded enterprises.[27] The first layer of exemption was on the machinery imported as part of the registered capital pledged by the foreign investors in the case of equity joint venture or wholly foreign-owned enterprises.[28] In the case of cooperative joint venture in selected sectors, tax exemption could be granted on imports that were part of the contributions by the foreign partners using foreign funds.[29] These selected sectors include energy exploration, basic construction of railway, highway, ports, forestry, animal husbandry and agriculture, deep-sea fishing, scientific research, education, medical treatment, and public health.

On top of that, there was the second layer of exemption granted on the import of machinery using the "total investment" fund or additional "total investment" fund by an equity joint venture or wholly foreign-owned enterprises.[30] Some Chinese officials point out that, while the tax exemption on the first layer is an international practice adopted by many countries, tax exemption on the second layer gives foreign-funded enterprises too many undue benefits.[31]

Beijing faces two choices in dealing with the tax exemption. One is to terminate the second layer exemption while keeping the first layer. This would significantly reduce the range of tax exemption for all imported machinery using the "total investment" fund. Tax exemption would only apply to the part of imported machinery financed by the pledged capital of the foreign investors, or to that contributed by foreign partners using foreign funds in the case of cooperative joint venture. The second choice is to scrap the two layers of exemption altogether and impose a customs duty on all imported machinery.

A reading of the published State Council notice on new Customs policies at the end of 1995, however, does not provide a clear picture of what exactly is Beijing's intention.[32] The wording of the notice seemed to be self-contradictory. On the one hand, it states that all imported machinery in the nation would be subjected to customs duty and VAT from 1 April 1996. On the other hand, termination of tax exemption related to imported machinery by foreign-funded enterprises is confined only to the exemption based on the concept of the "total investment" fund. There is no mention of the exemption of the first layer.

If Beijing's original decision were to scrap the second layer exemption only, then its negative effects on foreign investment would be quite limited. After all it is an "excessive" benefit by any international standard. Since Beijing announced the termination of the duty exemption, it has already twice granted grace periods to the foreign-funded enterprises set up before 1 April 1996. For those with a total investment of less than US$ 30 million, the exemption period was first extended to the end of 1996. For those with a total investment equal to or larger than US$ 30 million by 28 December 1995, the grace period was granted up to the end of 1997.[33] Later, in February 1997, Beijing extended the grace period for six more months to the foreign-funded enterprises falling into these two categories.[34]

If Beijing's original decision was however to terminate both layers of exemption altogether, then the cost of new investment projects, especially those capital-intensive ones, would increase considerably. This would happen even if one takes into consideration that China would in the meantime cut its average tariff rate by 30 per cent. Observers have pointed out that although the tariff slash covers nearly 5,000 items, there might be only a few hundred items that are relevant to the foreign investors. Investors in different industries may benefit to different degrees from the tariff reduction.[35] It should also be noted that the target of reducing the average tariff rate from 35.9 per cent to 23 per cent in 1996 is based on the simple average rate rather than the trade-weighted average rate. The scale of reduction might also be exaggerated since it does not take into account the reduced "provisional tariff", which had already been in operation in the previous years.

Reduction of VAT Rebates on Exports

Apart from the termination of tax exemption on the import of capital goods using the "total investment" fund, some exporting foreign-funded enterprises would also be affected by a reduction of VAT rebates on exports. Export rebate is an international practice. The rationale behind that is to avoid double taxing on export goods.[36] In the Chinese practice, the VAT rebate is payable to the exporting firm of the exported goods. The amount of the rebate equals the rebate rate times the export sales, up to the value of the purchase VAT.[37]

The purchase VAT is defined as VAT paid on raw materials or intermediate goods purchased for making the export goods where the exporting firm produces the exported goods. Where the exporting firm does not produce (or add value to) the exported goods, the purchase VAT is the VAT paid on the exported goods purchased from the local producer.

The export rebates come from the central government budget. Before the 1994 tax reform, the local governments shared 20 per cent of the cost. Under the new tax-sharing system introduced in 1994, the local governments would only pay a fixed amount based on the 1993 figures and would no longer contribute more as a proportion of the total rebates.[38]

China has already lowered its export rebate rates twice since 1994. When the new VAT system was introduced at the beginning of 1994, the rebate rates were set the same as the VAT rates: the 17 per cent basic rate and the 13 per cent preferential rate.[39] From 1 January 1996, however, three new rebate rates have been introduced. These are the 3 per cent rate for coal and agricultural products, the 6 per cent rate for products using agricultural products as raw materials and other products qualifying for the 13 per cent VAT preferential rate, and the nine-per cent rate for all other goods (Table A1.2).[40] A reduction of the VAT rebate rates usually means an increase of costs for exporting firms.

The changes in the rebate rates in 1995 and 1996 were due to the fact that the rebate rates were set too high in the first place in 1994. China adopted the export rebate as early as the mid-1980s. At that time though, instead of having two or three rebate rates, there were more than a hundred different rates applied on different products.[41] As the average rebate rate was around 10 per cent, the system was still viable.[42] On those grounds, we might regard the new rates introduced in 1996 as reasonably low and likely to continue to function in the future.

Although foreign-funded enterprises accounted for more than one third of China's total exports, the change of the VAT rebate rates might not have an immediate impact on most foreign-funded enterprises. This is because foreign-funded enterprises that were set up before 1 January 1994, unlike their Chinese counterparts, are not entitled to the export rebate in the first place.[43] And by 1995, more than 80 per cent of the foreign-funded enterprises in China had been registered before that date.[44]

How VAT Rebate Reduction Affects Foreign-Funded Firms

The new rebate rates would indeed affect the foreign-funded enterprises that were set up after 1 January 1994. These negative effects, however, might not be very serious either because of the following two factors.

First, all foreign-funded enterprises (like domestic exporting enterprises in some open zones) are still exempted from paying VAT on imported raw materials used for export processing. Many export processing foreign-funded enterprises do use imported raw materials. For those using Chinese raw materials, an alternative is to buy them via Hong Kong and report them as "imported materials". In fact, there has been a surge of such "re-import" via Hong Kong in recent years.[45]

Second, the old rebate rates in 1994 and 1995 were not viable. The arrears of rebates were Rmb 22.5 billion (34 per cent of the rebates claimed) in 1994 and were estimated to be Rmb 47.5 billion in 1995 (46 per cent of the rebates claimed).[46] Exporting firms would be unlikely to get a full rebate anyway even if the old rebate rates still prevailed. For foreign-funded enterprises that are entitled to the rebates, it might be a better choice to receive the rebates, albeit at a lower rate, under the new system. As Xiang Huai-cheng, Deputy Director of the State Administration Bureau of Taxation, promised in late 1995, China would clear the arrears of export rebates in two years' time.[47]

The new VAT rebate rates, therefore, are expected to affect mostly China's domestic exporting enterprises and it might have unfavourable effects on China's current account balance in the near future. In 1996 China's export only managed to grow 3 per cent, a remarkable slowdown compared to the previous year's 22.9 per cent growth. The trade surplus consequently ended up lower in 1996 amounting to US$ 16 billion.[48] This could be explained by the difficulties Chinese exporting firms are now facing: increases in domestic prices and interest rates, the stronger currency, and the reduction of export rebates.

2.4 FOR BETTER OR FOR WORSE

To summarize, the policy changes since 1994 have been in the direction of a level playing field for all firms. Official tax policies aim to treat firms of all ownership-types equally. This has been a significant switch from the earlier policy regimes.

Still Privileged

For foreign investors, the preferential tax policies that are still applicable after these policy adjustments are summarized in Table A1.3. They are divided into the following categories:

- Special rates: 15 per cent or 24 per cent as against the normal rate of 30 per cent;
- Tax holidays for corporate income tax;
- Rebates of corporate income tax for reinvestment;
- Special rates of withholding tax: zero per cent to 10 per cent as against the normal rate of 20 per cent;
- Deductions and exemptions of personal income tax;
- Rebate and exemptions of VAT and other turnover tax;
- Exemptions of import duties and VAT on imports;
- Export duties and VAT rebates on exports;
- Other tax exemptions (e.g. investment adjustment tax, urban maintenance and development tax).

Winners and Losers

There are of course winners or losers in the changes of tax policies discussed above. In the long term, however, it should be a blessing for most investors, both domestic and foreign, to have a more equal competition environment between indigenous enterprises and foreign-funded ones. The recent change in tax policies is a move toward a better investment environment in China.

The short-term effects of these policy changes are, however, not so certain. As shown in Table 2.2, in 1995, firms of different ownership-types still faced highly unequal burdens of sales-related taxes despite the unification of corporate income tax rates.

The state-owned sector was the only one whose share of sales-related taxes exceeded its share of added value. Share-holding companies, many of which are state-owned, were the only group where tax share equals its share of added value.

All the other sectors, except the "other" category, enjoyed a tax share lower than their share of added value. The foreign-funded firms' tax share was 25 per cent lower than their share of added value while the firms owned by Overseas Chinese had a tax share 43 per cent lower than their share of the added value.

Table 2.2 *Burdens of Sales-Related Taxes by Ownership (Unit: Rmb billions)*

1995	Sales Revenue	Per cent of Total	Added Value	Per cent of Total	Tax Paid	Per cent of Total
State-owned	2610.31	49	830.72	54	220.85	65
Collective-owned	1426.98	27	386.63	25	66.36	19
Share-Holding	269.76	5	77.61	5	16.36	5
Foreign-Funded	445.29	8	119.37	8	19.62	6
Overseas Chinese	456.97	9	108.81	7	14.38	4
Others	84.31	2	21.49	1	3.97	1
Total	5293.62	100	1544.61	100	341.54	100

Note: Sales-related taxes are various taxes and surcharges based on the firm's sales revenue value. They include value-added taxes, consumption taxes, urban maintenance surcharges, education surcharges, etc.

Source: *China Statistical Yearbook*, 1996.

Neither did the 1994 tax reform immediately unify the effective rates of sales-related taxation on firms of different ownership-types, as shown in Table 2.3. The effective rates of sales-related taxes, defined as the tax paid as a percentage of sales revenue, converged slightly for different ownership groups from 1990 to 1995.

Table 2.3 Effective Rates of Sales-Related Taxation

1990	Taxes Paid (billions Rmb)	Sales Revenue (billions Rmb)	Effective Rate (per cent)
1.State-Owned	111.50	1171.87	9.51
2.Collective-Owned	23.94	430.34	5.56
3.Others	3.16	77.10	4.10
Total	138.61	1679.31	8.25
1995	Sales-related Taxes Paid (billions Rmb)	Sales Revenue (billions Rmb)	Effective Rate (per cent)
1.State-Owned	220.85	2610.31	8.46
2.Collective-Owned	66.36	1426.98	4.65
3.Share-Holding	16.36	269.76	6.06
4.Foreign-Funded	19.62	445.29	4.41
5.Overseas Chinese	14.38	456.97	3.15
6.Others	3.97	84.31	4.71
7.Sum of 3, 4, 5 and 6 (equivalent to 3. in 1990)	54.33	1256.34	4.32
Total	341.54	5293.62	6.45

Notes:
1. The item "Overseas Chinese" in the statistics refers to firms owned by businesspersons from Hong Kong, Macao and Taiwan.
2. The taxation on sales includes sales-related taxes as in Table 2.2.

Source: *China Statistical Yearbook*, 1991 and 1996.

Rates for both state-owned firms and collective firms became lower while that for other firms as a whole became higher. The rates in 1995 nevertheless continued to vary significantly for different ownership groups. State-owned enterprises paid a rate nearly twice that which foreign-funded firms had to pay.

Changing Tides

As for foreign investors, even the Chinese side is not very sure whether or not the policy change would discourage FDI inflows. On the one hand, China claimed (or rather hoped) that large foreign investors would care more about their market shares and profit margins than about the preferential policies.[49] On the other hand, some studies show that preferential policies did play an important part in attracting FDI inflows, especially those from Hong Kong and Taiwan. For example, a State Statistical Bureau survey in 1994 showed that "preferential policies" were the second most important factor that foreign companies consider when investing in China. This was second only to the factor of "cheap labour" but ahead of the factor of "market potential".[50]

At a first glance, withdrawal of preferential tax policies and the macroeconomic slowdown since 1994 have already had their impact on the inflow of FDI in China. After the 1994 tax reform, the annual growth rate of the actual amount of FDI decreased from 23 per cent in 1994 to 12 per cent in 1995 and 16 per cent in 1996. Even the growth rate in 1994 was no match to those of the peak years in 1992 and 1993 when the actual amount of FDI was almost tripled each year. The total value of contracted FDI was less than US$ 70 billion in 1996, compared with the US$ 111 billion of the peak year of 1993.

To evaluate the effects of the policy change in the short term, two developments are worth watching. One is the changing weight of the investment from Hong Kong and Macao in China's total FDI inflow. As noted in Chapter 1, investment from Hong Kong and Macao has contributed more than half of China's FDI influx and a considerable portion of it has been funded by China's domestic sources. The other is the change of the structure of FDI source countries, especially the proportion of FDI from large Multi–national Firms (MNFs), which is supposed to be less sensitive to the preferential policy per se.

Chart 1.2 shows that the contribution of Hong Kong–Macao investment to the total FDI inflow has been on the wane since 1992. This trend could signal two positive effects of the policy adjustments in recent years. First, the "fake FDI" that aims to take advantage of the investor-oriented preferential policies may be curbed by the tax policy changes. Second, the value and share of FDI from other countries, especially of those initiated by large MNFs of the OECD countries, must be on rise.

According to the MOFTEC, 400 transitional corporations have made direct investment in China since 1992 with half of them entering the Chinese market for the first time in 1996. The majority of these multinational firms are from the United States, Japan, and the European Union countries. Over 200 of the top 500 firms listed in the US Fortune magazine have started their ventures in China.[51]

NOTES

1. See Lu D. (1994a), Chapter 4, for a more detailed discussion of China's Socialist Transformation in the 1950s.
2. The Central Committee of the CPC, "Resolution on Restructuring Economic System", *Renmin Ribao* [People's Daily], 22 October 1984.
3. See *Decision of the Central Committee of the CPC on Reform of the Economic Structure*, in the appendix of Liu and Wu eds (1986).
4. Hua Sheng et al., "A Decade of China's Reform: Looking Back, Reflection, and Prospect", *Jingji Yanjiu* [Economic Research], no. 9, September 1988, pp. 13–37; Shi Xiaomin and Liu Jirui, "Review on 'A Decade of China's Reform' ", *Jingji Yanjiu* [Economic Research], no. 2, 1989, pp. 11–33.
5. In Guangdong Province, for example, a typically contracted enterprise would be bound to increase its submission to the government on a 7 per cent annual rate in three years on the basis of its profits and taxes submitted in the contracted year. Of the profits surpassing the contracted submission, 80–90 per cent would go to the enterprise, and 10–20 per cent to the government. (*Jiefang Ribao* [Liberation Daily], Shanghai, China, 4 February 1988, p. 2).
6. Zhao Ziyang, "The Report on the Third Plenary of the 13th Central Committee of the CPC", *Renmin Ribao* [People's Daily], 28 October 1988.
7. *Shijie Jingji Daobao* [The World Economic Herald], Shanghai, China, 19 Dec. 1988, p. 15.
8. Wong et al. eds (1995).
9. *Almanac of China's Economy* (1985), Beijing, V: 19–20.
10. Lu (1994a), p. 156.
11. *Renmin Ribao* [People's Daily], 17 January 1990, p. 4.
12. For details of China's banking and financial system, see Gan (1995), Peebles (1991a, 1991b), the PBC (1994), Xie et al. (1992), Xie (1994), Yi (1994), Yu and Xie (1996), Wang (1991), World Bank (1990), and Zhu (1993).
13. Gan (1995).
14. Figures in this paragraph come from Gan (1995) and a news release of a Chinese official report on state enterprises appeared in *Lianhe Zaobao* [United Morning Post], Singapore, 23 December 1995.
15. *China Daily*, Beijing, 6 October 1996.
16. See Walder (1992) for a more detailed description of the bargaining relationships concerning the effective tax rates and financial support.
17. 'Outlines of the Ninth Five-Year Plan for National Economic and Social Development and the Long-term Target for the Year 2010', *Xinhua News Agency Daily Report*, 20 March 1996.
18. Reuter, *Straits Times*, Singapore, 25 December 1996, p. 12.
19. See Ma (1995).
20. Ma (1995) shows that, when the central government's priority projects are underinvested by the local banks, the central bank will have the ex post incentive to revise the credit ceiling upwards.
21. For a more detailed review of the 1994 tax reform, see Brudvig (1994).
22. There are still corporate income tax exemptions provided as part of the industrial policies and regional policies (see Chapters 3 and 4 for more details).
23. Xiang Huai-cheng, deputy director of China's State Administration of Taxation, said at the end of 1995 that policy changes in corporate tax were "high on our agenda". Such plans would, however, "usually take one, two or even three years to map out". *Asian Wall Street Journal*, Hong Kong, 29 November 1995.
24. More accurate wording should be "machinery and equipment, their parts and components, and other materials required for construction of sites and factories, or installation and reinforcement of the machinery". See "Measures of Customs of the PRC For Supervision, Tax Collection and Exemption On Imports and Exports of Foreign-Funded Enterprises" in *Zhonghua Renmin*

Gonghe Guo Haiguan Guanshui: Zhengce, Fagui, Shiwu, Shuize [Customs Duty Of PRC: Policy, Regulation, Practice and Tariff], Beijing: Chinese Customs 1994, pp. 54–57.

25. Du H. L.: "*Guanyu Touzi Zong-E*" [On "Total Investment Fund"], *Guoji Shangbao* [International Business], Beijing, 21 March 1996.
26. "Provisional Regulations of the State Administration for Industry and Commerce on the Ratio between the Registered Capital and Total Investment of Sino–foreign Joint Equity Enterprises" in *China Laws for Foreign Business: Business Regulation,* CCH Australia Ltd., 1993, pp. 6–554.
27. "Measures of Customs of the PRC For Supervision, Tax Collection and Exemption On Imports and Exports of Foreign-Funded Enterprises" in *Zhonghua Renmin Gonghe Guo Haiguan Guanshui: Zhengce, Fagui, Shiwu, Shuize* [Customs Duty Of PRC: Policy, Regulation, Practice and Tariff], Beijing, Chinese Customs 1994, pp. 54–57.
28. Item 1, Article 13 and Article 14 of the "Measures", ibid.
29. Article 15 of the "Measures", ibid.
30. Items 2 and 3, Article 13 of the "Measures", ibid.
31. Du H. L., ibid.
32. *Guoji Shang Bao* [International Business], Beijing, 29 December 1995.
33. *Guoji Shang Bao* [International Business], Beijing, 29 December 1995.
34. *China Daily,* Beijing, 2 February 1997, Business Weekly section.
35. *Business Times* (Singapore), 6 December 1995, p. 9.
36. World Bank (1988), p. 177.
37. "State Administration Bureau of Taxation: Notice On Export Rebates for Foreign-Funded Enterprises" in *Zhonghua Renmin Gonghe Guo Dui Wai Jingji Maoyi Hezuo Bu Wengao* [Gazette of Ministry of Foreign Trade and Economic Cooperation of the PRC], Beijing: MOFTEC, 1995, p. 60.
38. *Cai Zheng* [Public Finance], Beijing, 1994, no. 2, p. 20.
39. "Measures For Export Rebates and Tax Exemption" in *Zhonghua Renmin Gonghe Guo Dui Wai Jingji Maoyi Hezuo Bu Wengao* [Gazette of Ministry of Foreign Trade and Economic Cooperation of the PRC], Beijing: MOFTEC, 1994, no. 19, pp. 3–11.
40. "State Council Notice On Reducing Rates of Export Rebate" and "State Council Notice On Reduction of Export Rebate Rate and Enhanced Administration on Export Tax Rebate" in *Zhonghua Renmin Gonghe Guo Dui Wai Jingji Maoyi Hezuo Bu Wengao* [Gazette of Ministry of Foreign Trade and Economic Cooperation of the PRC], Beijing: MOFTEC, 1995, p. 81 and p. 68.
41. Wang S. G. (1993), *Zhongguo de Zengzhi Shui he Yingye Shui* [China's VAT and Business Tax], Shanghai: Li Xin Accounting, p. 122. Also Liu X. D ed. (1993), pp. 242–252.
42. Xiang Huai-cheng, Deputy Director of the State Administration Bureau of Taxation in *Guoji Jingmao Xiaoxi* [International Trade News] Beijing, 30 November 1995, p. 1.
43. "State Administration Bureau of Taxation Notice On Export Rebates for foreign-funded enterprises" in *Zhonghua Renmin Gonghe Guo Dui Wai Jingji Maoyi Hezuo Bu Wengao* [Gazette of Ministry of Foreign Trade and Economic Cooperation of the PRC], Beijing: MOFTEC, 1995 p. 60; also "Would Preferential Policies for Foreign Investors Be Abolished?" in *Zhongguo Wai Zi* [China's Foreign Investment], Beijing, 1996, no 1. See also *Business China,* the Economist Intelligence Unit, Hong Kong, 13 November 1995, p. 2.
44. *State China Statistical Yearbook 1995,* Beijing: State Statistical Bureau, 1995, p. 558.
45. *Guoji Shang Bao* [International Business], Beijing, 10 November 1995, p. 3.
46. *Jinrong Shibao* [Financial Times], Beijing, 23 December 1995, p. 5. Also Wu, C., *Muqian Wuoguo Chukou Tui Shui Cunzai de Wenti Ji Duice* [Problems and Solutions in Export Rebate in China] in *Guoji Maoyi Wenti* [International Trade Journal], Beijing, 1995 no. 11, pp. 13–16.
47. *Guoji Jingmao Xiaoxi* [International Trade News] Beijing, 30 November 1995, p. 1.
48. AFP, Reuter, *Staits Times,* Singapore, 23 December 1996 and 4 January 1997.

49. *Guoji Jingmao Xiaoxi* [International Trade News], Beijing, 1 February 1996.
50. The survey was conducted by the Urban Social and Economic Survey Division of the SSB on 1,500 foreign-funded enterprises randomly drawn from the population of all foreign-funded enterprises in China. The recent survey showed that 84 per cent, 56 per cent and 51 per cent of the foreign-funded enterprises ranked cheap labour, preferential policies, and market potential respectively as the most important factor for their investment in China. (Source: Ren Cai-fang, head of the Urban Social and Economic Survey Division, seminar given in the Institute of East Asian Political Economy, Singapore, June 1996.)
51. *China Business,* Beijing, 27 December 1996, p. 5.

3. Region-Oriented Policies

3.1 FROM INLAND AUTARKIES TO COASTAL ZONES

Geographically China's vast mountainous inland areas are rich in mineral resources but far less accessible than the country's coastal areas. In modern Chinese history, the coastal areas developed the first batch of modern industries and infrastructure for modern commercial activities. Since the founding of the PRC in 1949, China's regional development strategy has experienced two distinctive periods.

The Inward-Looking Regional Strategy in the Mao Era[1]

When the CPC government started its industrialization programme in the early 1950s, it regarded the imbalance of development between the coastal and inland regions as "irrational". At the time the newly founded People's Republic of China faced the political and economic sanctions of the Western camp and was fighting a war against the US and its allies in the Korea Peninsula. The government was therefore anxious to develop economic independence and prepare itself for possible foreign military invasions. Against this backdrop, China adopted an inward-looking regional development strategy in her industrialization programme.[2]

The first feature of this strategy was to ensure economic independence by pursuing a nationwide self-sufficiency. The location of coastal industries in the pre-PRC history was justified by their convenient links to international markets. This was no longer desirable for the self-sufficient independent economy the PRC government was attempting to build. Therefore the First Five-Year Plan (1953–57) laid down that the industrial capital construction should locate industries close to sources of raw materials and fuel or to areas of consumption. Capital construction should gradually change the "irrational distribution of industry and develop the economy of backward areas". During the First Five-Year Plan period, nearly 56 per cent of the state investment in fixed assets went to the inland regions.

The second feature of the strategy was its emphasis on national defence. According to the First Five-Year Plan, the location of new projects should comply with the need to strengthen national defence. This principle evolved into a policy of systematically relocating China's modern industries in inland regions in the 1960s. Awake to the escalating of the Vietnam War, the CPC leaders at a meeting in 1964 divided China into three fronts in the event of a possible full-scale foreign invasion. The "first front", the most vulnerable area to invasion, refers to the eastern coastal provinces and the northern regions bordering the Soviet Union. The "third front" refers to the inland mountainous regions, which could serve as the stronghold in a prolonged war against invaders. The "second front" refers to the areas between the first and the third fronts. Based on a strategic plan to prepare the nation for an overall self-defence war, both China's Third and Fourth Five-Year Plans (1966–70 and 1971–75) concentrated massive capital and human resources on the "third front construction".[3]

The third feature of the strategy was its promotion of a "cellular economy", which consisted of small, self-sufficient units operating at the regional level.[4] Unlike in the former Soviet Union where local "empire building" of economic self-sufficiency was discouraged, all provinces and regions in Mao's China were encouraged to develop their "comprehensive and independent" economies. Mao rejected the principle of regional specialization and exchange in national economic planning. Instead he favoured regional autonomy and self-reliance. One factor behind this attitude was Mao's dislike of rigid Soviet-style bureaucracy resulting from large-scale economic planning and coordination among regions. A profound belief in mass mobilization and "people's initiative" made Mao enthusiastically promote in the late 1950s the semi-military "People's Communes", which featured very little division of labour and an egalitarian distribution of income. The cellular-economy policy was also defence-oriented. It was believed that building hundreds of self-sufficient cellular economies around China would provide the country with the best chance to survive and win a large-scale war against foreign invasion.

The Coast-Oriented Development in the Post-Mao Era

Mao's death in 1976 marked the end of the Cultural Revolution and the beginning of a new era. Two years later at the landmark Third Plenary of the Eleventh CPC Central Committee, the reform-minded leaders headed by Deng Xiaoping got the upper hand in the Party's leadership. Since then the Party has focused on economic development rather than socialist revolutions. The Chinese economy has hence embarked on market-oriented reforms.

Deng and his colleagues understood that if China continued adhering to Mao's principle of self-sufficiency the country would never be able to modernize its economy. Foreign technology and capital were crucial to

China's modernization efforts. To open the Chinese economy to the world, China must befriend the international community and maintain a favourable and peaceful international environment. A series of diplomatic efforts, including normalizing diplomatic relations with the US in 1979, successfully paved the way for China to benefit from participating in the world economy. The Maoist national defence strategy became obsolete. The policy of self-sufficiency gave way to the open-door policy. With these changes, it was inevitable that the regional development strategy turned around from being inward looking to become coast-oriented. From Chart 3.1 we can observe clearly the reversion of regional development strategy during the Fifth Five-Year Plan period (1976–80). The coastal region started to become the central stage of China's economic development as soon as China commenced the market-oriented reforms.[5]

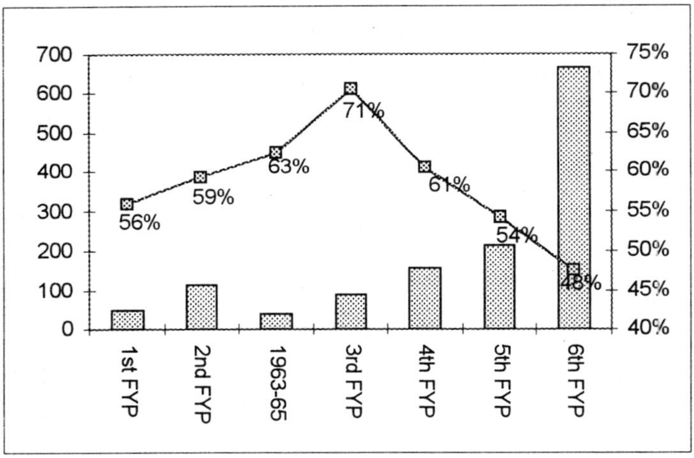

Notes:

1. Periods of Five-Year Plans are: 1953–57 (First FYP); 1958–62 (Second FYP); 1965–70 (Third FYP); 1971–75 (Fourth FYP); 1976–80 (Fifth FYP); and 1981–85 (Sixth FYP).
2. The figure for the Sixth FYP is total investment while the figures for other periods are investment in the state sector. Before 1980, the investment in non-state sectors was negligibly small.

Source: *China Statistical Yearbook*, various issues and Jia and Tisdell (1996).

Chart 3.1 Investment in Fixed Assets (Rmb billion) and Shares of Inland Regions (1953–1985)

3.2 THE "VANGUARD OF REFORM"

Among China's preferential policies, the region-oriented ones are most manifest in the official approach toward foreign investment. In particular, the central government has granted a series of economic privileges to those doing business in the Special Economic Zones (SEZs) since the early 1980s. Thanks to these privileges, few countries have the variety of regional business environments as exists in China.

China's five SEZs are situated in the country's southeast coast area. Three of them, Shenzhen, Shantou and Zhuhai, are in Guangdong province, which is bordering Hong Kong. The Xiamen SEZ belongs to Fujian province, which faces Taiwan across the strait. The largest SEZ is the whole of Hainan province, China's largest island. Except for Hainan, all the SEZs were set up in 1980. Table 3.1 gives the details on their set-up date, area and boundary.

The Experimental Grounds

Economic reform started in 1979 as the Chinese leaders' pragmatic response to the then critical economic situation after the ending of the chaotic "Great Proletarian Cultural Revolution (1966–1976)". As discussed in Chapter 1, facing ideological constraints and resistance from the old system, the reformers had to take a "trial-and-error" approach.

An important strategy that has minimized and diversified the political and economic risks of reform was called the policy of "*shidian*", which literally means the "experimental grounds". Under this policy, reform schemes should be first experimented with in selected enterprises, sectors or regions. If a scheme works at the local level, the top leadership would promote it in the whole nation. If it does not, the leadership would bury it without inviting too much political fuss.

As "experiment grounds" for the open-door policy and market-oriented reforms, four localities, namely Shenzhen, Zhuhai, Shantou and Xiamen, were selected as the earliest SEZs between 1979 and 1980. These zones became the first state-approved capitalist enclaves to lead the nation on her long march of the market-oriented reform. At a time when China's centrally planned economy was largely shunned by the world market, the emergence of those zones was a breakthrough in launching China's market-oriented reform.

Blessed with greater freedom to experiment local reforms, the SEZs have always been at the forefront of China's economic reform. For instance, the central government adopted regulations in November 1987 to allow Shenzhen and Hainan to begin a new leasing programme in an attempt to make better use of real estates. Consequently, a property market boom emerged in these areas when the concept of real estate transaction was still alien to the rest of the country.

Table 3.1 *Change of Boundaries of the Special Economic Zones*

SEZ	Year of Set-up and Expansion	Area (sq. km.)	Change of Boundary
Shenzhen	1980	327.5	Including Luohu, Futian and Nanshan districts, but excluding Baoan and Longgang districts. From 1992 onwards, foreign-funded enterprises in Baoan district (751.6 sq. km.) could enjoy the SEZ policies
Zhuhai	1980	15.16	
	1988	121	Including a part of the Xiangzhou district bordering Macao. From 1993 onwards, foreign-funded enterprises in the western districts including Doumen County, Sanzao, Pingsha, Hongqi, Zhuhai Harbour districts could enjoy the SEZ policies.
Shantou	1981	1.6	Longhu section
	1984	52.6	Longhu and Guangao sections
	1991	234	Whole of Shantou city including Longhu, Shengping, Jinyuan and Dahao districts but excluding Chenghai County, Nanao County and Chaoyang City which are under Shantou's administration
Xiamen	1980	2.5	Huli section
	1984	130	Whole of Xiamen Island including Huli, Kaiyuan, Siming and Gulangyu districts but excluding Jimei and Xinglin districts and Tongan County which are under Xiamen's administration. From 1989 onwards, parts of the Jimei and Xinglin districts became Taiwan Investment Zone
Hainan	1988	33,907	Whole of Hainan Island

Source: *Statistics Year Books* of respective SEZs.

Windows to the Outside World

Beyond being the vanguard of domestic reforms, the SEZs have also spearheaded China's open-door policy through the 1980s to the 1990s. Metaphorically described as China's "windows" to the outside world, the SEZs have played an important role in introducing foreign technology, capital, and management into the country. The choice of the SEZs as the "windows" is due to the sheer fact that they are geographically adjacent to Hong Kong, Macao and Taiwan and are located in the areas which are home towns of some 21 million overseas Chinese in the region.[6] It was expected that cultural affinity and preferential policies would be the major attraction for overseas Chinese to invest in the SEZs.

The open-door policy worked quite well in the SEZs after several years of the start-up period. The SEZs soon became the top destination of foreign direct investment (FDI) in the country around the mid-1980s, when these zones accounted for about 30 per cent of actualized FDI in China in 1984. For the reasons we would discuss later, this ratio has dropped in the 1990s. Nevertheless in 1994, the cities of Shenzhen, Zhuhai, Shantou, Xiamen and Hainan province, with less than 1 per cent of China's population and only 3 per cent of China's GDP, hosted about 17 per cent of the actualized FDI in the nation and made 22 per cent of China's exports.[7] Partially as a result of these zones' geographic location and their affinity with overseas Chinese, FDI structure in China has been heavily geared to Hong Kong and Taiwan as the major source economies. During 1979–1993 Hong Kong and Taiwan commited themselves to about 85 per cent of the contracted FDI in China.[8]

Setting up the SEZs has another important political implication. It serves the strategic need in China's cause of reclaiming her sovereignty over Hong Kong and Macao in the late 1990s and Taiwan in the future. The rapid economic growth in the SEZs would certainly help to narrow the gap in living standards between these regions and their bordering Chinese territories. The nominal per capita GDP in Shenzhen and Zhuhai for example, was around US$ 2,000 in 1994, much higher than the national average of US$ 440, although still far less than the US$ 21,500 of Hong Kong and US$ 15,800 of Macao. The growing volume of trade and investment also facilitated the economic integration between mainland China and Hong Kong or Taiwan.

3.3 PROLIFERATION OF OPEN ZONES

Ironically, it was the success of the SEZs itself that brought about the downfall of the SEZs' fortunes. Inspired by the early achievement of the SEZs, the central government decided to promote the SEZ model in more regions by setting up an echelon of open zones. These zones would enjoy a variety of preferential policies similar to those applied in the SEZs. With the proliferation of open zones since the mid-1980s, the SEZs began to face more and more competition from other coastal or even inland provinces in attracting new FDI.

The SEZs reached their heyday in 1984, the year when the patriarch leader, Deng Xiaoping, visited Shenzhen and Zhuhai and praised the achievements of the SEZs. In 1984 and 1985 the central government created 14 coastal open cities ranging from Dalian in the northeastern province of Liaoning to Beihai in the southern province of Guangxi and the Coastal Economic Open Zones. The Economic and Technological Development Zones were set up within these open cities where foreign investors could enjoy preferential policies which were almost the same as those in the SEZs. In 1990, the Pudong New Area was set up in Shanghai. The Pudong New Area not only enjoys all the preferential policies of the SEZs, but also has even more freedom in allowing foreign investors in areas like retailing and financial sectors.

Another new wave of opening-up started in 1992 shortly after Deng Xiaoping's South China tour, when he made personal appeals to the central and local leaderships for more rapid economic reforms.[9] Open zones were extended to inland provinces in the form of the Inland Open Cities, the Economic and Technological Development Zones within the Inland Open Cities, the Border Open Cities, etc.

By 1995, there were 11 kinds of open zones formally approved by the State Council.[10] They included:

- The five Special Economic Zones (SEZs), set up in 1980 and 1988;
- The Pudong New Area, set up in 1990;
- The 33 Economic and Technological Development Zones, set up in 1984, 1992 and 1994 (including the Suzhou–Singapore Industrial Park);
- The 14 Coastal Open Cities, set up in 1984;
- The seven Coastal Economic Open Zones, set up in 1985, 1988, 1990 and 1992;
- The 24 Inland Open Cities, set up in 1992;
- The 13 Border Open Cities, set up in 1992;

- The 13 Border Economic Cooperation Zones, set up in 1992;
- The 13 Bonded Areas, set up from 1990 to 1992;
- The 52 High-Tech Industry Development Zones, set up in 1991 and 1992;
- The 11 State Holiday Resort Zones, set up in 1992.

These open zones, however, do not have exactly the same special policies as enjoyed by the SEZs. They have different functions and receive different degrees of preferences. For instance, to encourage foreign investment in the tourist industry is the goal of the State Holiday Resort Zones. The Border Economic Cooperation Zones set up in the Border Open Cities aim at promoting border trade. The Bonded Areas are for development of entrepot trade while the High-Tech Industry Development Zones give tax concessions only to those qualified hi-tech enterprises in terms of products, expenditure on research and development. It seems inevitable that the proliferation of these open zones would divert foreign investors' attention to the SEZs.

3.4 NO LONGER THAT SPECIAL

There are three major categories of special policies for the SEZs and the other open zones: (a) concession on corporate income tax; (b) concession on customs duties and value-added taxes (VAT) on exports and imports; and (c) local government's authority of economic management. Tables A1.4 and A1.5, respectively, provide comparisons of the preferential policies in categories (a) and (b) for foreign investors applied nationwide, in the SEZs and other open zones. Most policies in Table A1.5 were valid up to the end of 1993. More recent policy adjustments are reflected in Tables A1.1 and A1.2.

Corporate Income Tax

Unifying the previously various rates of nationwide corporate income tax to a uniform rate was a goal of the 1994 tax reform. The reform set the normal corporate income tax rate at 30 per cent for all enterprises, including foreign-funded enterprises and domestic enterprises. Region-oriented preferential tax policy, however, still remains.

The foreign-funded enterprises operating in the SEZs have for years enjoyed a special rate of 15 per cent. In recent years, this special-rate benefit has been extended to equity joint ventures engaged in construction of ports and docks, and qualified foreign-funded banks nationwide. Beijing has also granted the special rate to all "production-oriented" (that is, "non-service") foreign-funded enterprises in the Economic and Technological Development Zones, Pudong New Area and Bonded Areas. Meanwhile the high-tech enterprises in the High-Tech Industry Development Zones and selected "production-oriented" foreign-funded enterprises in the Coastal Open Cities, the Inland Open Cities and the Coastal Economic Open Zones also qualify for such a special rate.

There is another special corporate income tax rate of 24 per cent. The rate applies to all "production-oriented" foreign-funded enterprises in the Coastal Open Cities, the Inland Open Cities and the Coastal Economic Open Zones. The benefit is also for all foreign-funded enterprises in the Border Open Cities, the Border Economic Cooperation Zones, and the State Holiday Resort Zones.

To various degrees, foreign-funded enterprises in certain businesses have enjoyed the benefits in exemption from or reduction in corporate income taxes in the SEZs and other open zones. In recent years, these benefits have no longer been restricted to these zones. The same rules on the benefits such as "two years of exemption and three years of reduction by half" in corporate income taxes for certain businesses apply to foreign-funded enterprises all over the nation. There is also little difference in respect of granting further reduction for "export-oriented" and "technologically-advanced" foreign-funded enterprises (see Table A1.4 for details).

The remaining attractive points the SEZs have now are the types of enterprises that are qualified for the tax concession. Besides the "production oriented" foreign-funded enterprises, the foreign-funded enterprises in the service sector and all domestic enterprises (both "production-oriented" and in the service sector) inside the SEZs also qualify for the special rate of 15 per cent. (The rate would be 20 per cent should those enterprises remit the profit outside the SEZ.) There is also a period of tax exemption and reduction for the service business (for details see Tables A1.3 and A4).

Customs Duties and Value-Added Taxes

The SEZs have also lost ground in their privileged concessions on customs duties and VAT on imports. Outside the open zones, some selected foreign-funded enterprises can get concessions on customs duties and VAT for a restricted list of equipment. In quite a few open zones, foreign-funded enterprises and even domestic enterprises and institutions have had similar tax concessions as their counterparts in the SEZs.

The concessions of customs duties and VAT have applied to a wide range of imports: from equipment and materials for infrastructure construction, production, technological renovation and export, to vehicles and office equipment. Until 1996, the SEZs enjoyed exclusive tax policies on imports of commodities to be sold inside their borders. Up to an approved amount, most of these commodities were only liable to half of the customs duties and were exempted from VAT. Table A1.5 gives a summary of these concessions. However, as we shall discuss in the next section, there have been major adjustments in concessions on customs duties and VAT on imports since 1994, which in fact reduced even further the advantage of the SEZs and other open zones relative to other non-open zone areas.

Table 3.2 Approval Limits of Different Authorities Toward Investment Projects of Equity Joint Ventures and Wholly Foreign-Owned Enterprises

Approval Limits (Project Value)	Authorities
US$ 30 million	• The governments of the five SEZs • The nine coastal province-level governments: Fujian, Guangdong, Guangxi, Hebei, Jiangsu, Liaoning, Shandong, Shanghai Zhejiang • Cities that are under the direct supervision of the State Council and are located in the coastal provinces: Dalian, Guangzhou, Nanjing, Ningbo, Qingdao, Shenyang
US$ 20 million	Tianjin Municipality
US$ 10 million	• Other province-level governments • Certain important ministries, such as Ministries of Metallurgical Industry, Water Resources, Energy, and Agriculture • Cities that are under the direct supervision of the State Council and are not located in the coastal provinces: Chongqing, Changchun, Harbin, Wuhan and Xian • Beijing Municipality, with approval right for US$ 30 million in certain designated industries
US$ 5 million	Other Open Cities: Beihai, Fuqing, Fuzhou, Kunshan, Lianyungang, Nantong, Qinghuangdao, Weihai, Wenzhou, Yantai, Yingkou, Zhanjiang

Note: In 1997, Chongqing City became a province-level municipality.

Source: Trade Development Board, *Trade Investment Guide: China,* Singapore: Arthur Anderson, 1993.

Local Policies

Besides the tax concession, the governments in the SEZs used to enjoy privileged authorities in various aspects of local economic management. Most of these privileged rights, however, have been extended to other open cities in recent years. For instance:

- After the SEZs, the Coastal and Inland Open Cities have been given the authority to approve foreign investment projects up to US$ 30 million while the approval limit for other provinces is US$ 10 million only.[11] For more details of the approval limits, see Table 3.2.
- Shenzhen and Xiamen are two of the 14 "*jihua dan lie shi*" (cities under the direct supervision of the State Council).[12] The other 12 cities under this category are Harbin, Shenyang, Changchun, Dalian, Qingdao, Xian, Wuhan, Ningbo, Chongqing, Guangzhou, Nanjing and Chengdu. They can directly deal with the central government (instead of the provinces) to arrange their planned targets, such as the share of fiscal revenue to be submitted, the size of credit quota for bank loans, and the size of total investment.
- Following Shenzhen, Shanghai and some other selected Coastal Open Cities have been authorized by Beijing to set up stock exchanges and foreign currency swap centres after the late 1980s. Until recent years, foreign banks could only open branches in the five special economic zones and Shanghai. The People's Bank of China announced in June 1992 that it would allow foreign banks to open branches in seven more coastal cities, ranging from Dalian in the northeast to Canton, upriver from Hong Kong. The policy change was implemented in 1994 when China enacted new banking regulations that allow foreign banks to expand their banking businesses beyond the SEZs.[13] Similar policy adjustment has happened to foreign companies' retail business in China. Since 1994, outlets of foreign supermarkets and departmental stores have been allowed to operate beyond the SEZs.

3.5 FURTHER EROSION OF PRIVILEGES

Since 1994, Beijing has introduced a series of reform measures to the national tax system, central and local fiscal relationships and the foreign exchange system. These measures have in the following aspects eroded the basis of some important regional privileges.

(1) Before 1994, corporate income taxes paid by foreign-funded enterprises were a revenue item shared by the central and local governments. Granting tax concessions to the foreign-funded enterprises was therefore not a costly policy for the local government. The new tax assignment system introduced in 1994 has assigned the corporate income tax revenue collected from most foreign-funded enterprises fully to the local government budget. For the sake of their own fiscal revenue, the local governments (including those of the SEZs) would thus have less incentive to grant tax holidays to foreign-funded enterprises.[14]

(2) The new tax assignment system has introduced the same formula for dividing the fiscal revenue between the central and all local governments. This has replaced the old tax regime that gave more favourable treatment to the regions such as Guangdong and Fujian provinces. As a consequence, in 1994, there was a sharp increase in the SEZs' contributions of fiscal revenue to the central and provincial governments. For example, by the end of 1994, of Shenzhen city's Rmb 4.7-billion accumulated submission of fiscal revenue to the central and provincial governments, most was collected in 1994.[15]

(3) The scheme of foreign exchange retention for export firms was abolished in the 1994 foreign exchange reform. Foreign trade companies in the SEZs used to enjoy a higher ratio of foreign exchange retention, which was another privilege of doing business in the SEZs. They are now required to sell all their foreign exchange earnings from export to the authorized banks and buy foreign exchange from the latter when they import.

(4) As summarized in Tables A1.1 and A1.2, there have been major adjustments in concessions on customs duties and VAT on imports since 1994. For instance, the exemption of the customs duty and VAT for the imports of automobiles and office equipment was removed in 1994 and 1995.[16] From 1 April 1996, there has been no more exemption of customs duties and VAT on import of machinery by foreign-funded enterprises set up after the date. These same rules apply to enterprises or institutions in the SEZs, without exception. Moreover, from 1 January 1996, even the imported goods to be sold within the SEZs are no longer qualified for reduction of customs duties or exemptions of VAT. The amount of duty-free imports of machinery or raw materials in the five SEZs and the Pudong New Area have also been subject to a quota since July 1995. The quota will be reduced by 20 per cent each year until the year 2000 when the tax exemption is eliminated.[17]

There is more in the pipeline. On the one hand, Beijing is likely to reject the request of the SEZs for extending the Bonded Area (the area outside the national customs) to cover the whole of the SEZs, on the ground that "preferential policy" would no longer be granted on a regional basis. On the other hand, Beijing is expected to give more autonomy to western inland provinces for exploitation and export of their abundant mineral resources. The central government may also pump more investment funds into the Yangtze River Delta, the upland of the Pudong New Area in Shanghai.

Table 3.3 *Per Capita GDP and Average Annual Urban Wages in Selected Cities and Provinces (1993)*

City (province)	GDP per-capita (Rmb)	Average Annual Urban Wage (Rmb)
Lainyungang	2,191	2,855
Harbin	3,968	2,936
Xian	2,925	2,999
Hainan	2,916	3,138
Shenyang	6,116	3,346
Fuzhou	4,142	3,356
Wuhan	4,674	3,533
Tianjin	6,037	4,003
Shantou	3,196	4,371
Beijing	8,216	4,523
Xiamen	9,234	5,544
Shanghai	11,673	5,650
Guangzhou	11,377	6,342
Zhuhai	21,058	8,129
Shenzhen	14,019	8,145
All-China	**2,644**	**3,371**

Source: *Statistical Yearbook of China 1994,* Beijing: Chinese Statistics, 1994; *Yanhai Kaifang Chengshi, Jingji Tequ, Jihua Danlie Shi Tongji Ziliao Huibian* [Statistics on Coastal Open Cities, SEZs and Cities Under Direct Supervision of the State Council], Xiamen: Xiamen Statistics Bureau, 1994.

Fading Attractions

The above developments have greatly reduced the SEZs' attractiveness to foreign direct investment. Besides losing privileged policy treatment, the two earliest SEZs, Shenzhen and Zhuhai, have obviously suffered from the pressure of increasing wages and escalating costs relative to other parts of the nation (Table 3.3). For Hainan, the lack of a strong manufacturing base and a strong export potential has impeded economic growth. The 1992-1993 boom of the Hainanese economy was highly dependent on its real estate sector development, which has been badly hit by Beijing's austere monetary policy after 1994.[18]

As illustrated in Chart 3.2, compared with the peak year of 1984, the share of the SEZs in terms of actualized foreign direct investment in the nation decreased from 30 per cent to 11 per cent in 1995. The year 1995 also marked the first drop in the amount of actualized FDI in these zones. The full impact is yet to be felt if we take into account the time lag between the changes in investment environment and the changes in FDI actually utilized. The slowdown of the FDI inflow points to a gloomy prospect for the SEZs' GDP growth and exports in the coming years.

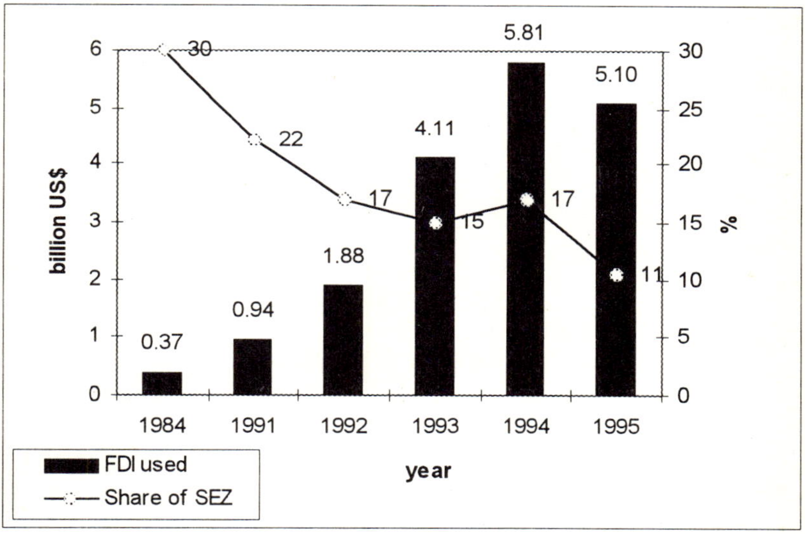

Source: *Almanac of China's Foreign Economic Relations*, Beijing, various issues.

Chart 3.2 FDI Actually Utilized in the SEZs and Its Share in China

3.6 POLICIES AT THE CROSSROADS

There are two important factors that explain the success of SEZs in the past: the geographic proximity to Hong Kong and Taiwan and the special policies granted by the central government. While the connection with Hong Kong will still be important, the effect of the special policies has first been weakened gradually during the spread of open zones and economic reform throughout the nation and then more seriously by new reform measures put forward since 1994. That is because the main political-economic factors that justified the exclusive preferential policies for the SEZs in the early 1980s no longer exist nowadays.

No More Necessary

In the initial stage of reform and opening, it was important for Beijing's reform-minded leaders to make sure that the whole nation would see the benefits of the new policies. Therefore it was in their interests to provide "preferential policies" to the "*shidian* (experimental-ground)" enterprises, sectors and regions. Meanwhile, when China was still a tightly controlled central-planned economy, those "*shidian*" regimes had to receive special autonomy to carry out local experiments of market-oriented reforms.

After more than 15 years of successful economic reforms, Deng Xiaoping's policy of market-oriented reform has become the consensus in the Party and its leadership. As various open zones have proliferated all over the nation and the door of the whole Chinese market has been flung open to foreign investors, the SEZs are apparently no longer the only "windows" to the world economy.

By the mid-1990s, China's economic reform also seems to have reached the stage where some of the hardest problems, such as reform of the state-owned enterprise and the social welfare system, have to be addressed. The experience from the newly developed SEZs might not be relevant to other old industrial cities where the bulk of state-owned enterprises are situated. Indeed China still needs experimental grounds for the final transition to a full-fledged market economy. There is, however, no good reason to confine such grounds to the five SEZs, especially if "experimenting" means they can enjoy "preferential policies" to the exclusion of other parts of the nation.

Too Costly to Keep

On the other hand, the social-economic costs of maintaining the region-oriented "preferential-policy" structure have become increasingly heavier. Any economic privilege is vested with economic rents, which invite rent-seeking activities. For instance, Deng Xiaoping's call in 1992 for a more speedy pace of reform and opening up led to a period of ill-planned and under-funded zone-creating drive. Through 1992 and the first half of 1993 more than 1,400 "economic development zones" were set up nationwide (without the central government's authorization) by local officials anxious to upgrade their regimes to enjoy "preferential policies". In a nationwide retrenchment, Beijing had to close down more than 1,200 unauthorized open zones in 1993-94.[19] These dramatic changes led to a huge waste of resources.

Special policies for the SEZs and coastal open cities have also aroused bitter feelings from other provinces, especially those in the interior parts of China. According to their opinions, special policies are more necessary in poor provinces to speed up their development processes. For instance, although Shenzhen received little direct investment from the central government, domestic investment from enterprises of other provinces poured into the SEZ to take advantage of the special policies. There were debates on whether Shenzhen's boom riding on the back of domestic capital was cost-effective for the nation as a whole.[20] Abolishing the special policies for SEZs is also a useful card for the post-Deng leadership in winning the support of the majority of the 30 provinces and autonomous regions.

Conflicting Interests

Taking away privileges from vested interests is, however, not an easy job. In the summer of 1995, debates over the SEZ privileges became heated. Li Youwei, the mayor of Shenzhen, led a media campaign against a Chinese scholar Hu Angang's view that the SEZ privileges should be abolished.[21] These debates were publicized at a time when the central government was preparing the Ninth Five-Year Plan (FYP) (1996–2000). The views presented in the debates might reflect the disagreement among Beijing's policy-makers over the regional distribution of the central government's investment and the future of the region-oriented preferential policy.

Another sign of confrontation was the report that the Party chief of Guangdong province was criticized at a high-level meeting for failing to toe the line of the central government to phase out the "preferential policies" for coastal regions (including SEZs).[22] In the autumn of 1995, the deputy secretary general of the State Planning Commission told reporters that the tax rate should be the same for Chinese and foreign companies, and that many of the financial advantages that make the special economic zones more attractive than other parts of China would be abolished in the foreseeable future.[23]

Beijing has nevertheless been handling the issue tactfully. Jiang Zhemin, the Party General Secretary, has ostensibly denied any abrupt cut-off of the special policies by promising the so-called "three-no-change" in his tour to the SEZs in 1994. Namely, there would be no change in the central government's resolution to build up the SEZs, no change in the function of the SEZs in the nation, and no change in the principal policies for SEZs.[24] He reiterated the "three-no-change" promise again during his visit to the SEZs at the end of 1995[25]. This notion, however, is ambiguous and can still be subject to different interpretations. In reality, the SEZs saw their privileges being gradually eroded in recent years, especially after a series of new reform measures were carried out in 1994. Some preferences that were previously exclusive to the SEZs have now been made available to other areas.

Changing Wind

In the Ninth Five-Year Plan promulgated in April 1996, the central government clearly signalled the change in state regional policies. The Plan mapped out several measures to support economic development in the central and west China.[26]

First, in state investment plans, the government would give priority to resource extraction projects and infrastructure constructions in the central and west China. The state would guide resource-related processing industries and labour-intensive industries to resettle in the inland regions. Second, the government would "rationalize" the prices of resource-related products so as to "enhance central and west China's self-development capacities". Third, the central government would develop a regulated financial transfer payment system to raise funds for inland development. The percentage of financial assistance to the inland regions in the state budget should also gradually increase. Fourth, the central government would accelerate the pace of reform and opening up in the inland regions and guide more foreign investors to these regions. More state policy-related loans would also be earmarked for central and west China, especially for impoverished areas. Finally, the government would take measures to encourage interregional economic cooperation and exchanges of capital, labour and technology.

A market economy thrives on fair and free competition. This means no region should be given undue special privileges. As China is rapidly moving towards a full-fledged market economy, the region-oriented "preferential policies" must be reformed. The SEZs will eventually lose their special treatment and rely more on their own natural comparative advantages based on their geographical location, infrastructure, natural and human resources, and their particular industrial mix. Meanwhile China has become more open to the world and is facing a huge task of transforming itself into an integrated part of the international economy. To accomplish the task, it is necessary to develop a set of internationally compatible fair-play rules for the domestic economy. Adjustment to China's region-oriented policy is inevitable and has already been in process.

NOTES

1. Mao Zedong (or Mao Tse-tung) (1893–1976) was the CPC's top leader from 1935 to 1976. The Mao Era of the PRC refers to the period from 1949–1976.

2. Jia and Tisdell (1996).
3. Zhao (1989), pp. 171–185.
4. Donnithorne (1972).
5. For a more detailed discussion of regional disparity in post-reform China, see Jia and Tisdell (1996) and Weinstein (1996).
6. *Yearbook of the Ethnic Chinese Economy*, Beijing: China Social Sciences Press, 1994.
7. See *Jingji Ribao* [Economic Daily], Beijing, 3 July, 1995; and *Te Qu Jingji* [SEZ Economy], Shenzhen, June 1995.
8. *Jingji Yanjiu Cankao* [Information for Economic Research], Beijing, 12 October 1994.
9. In February 1992, Deng Xiaoping visited several cities in South China and made a series of important speeches on economic reform and national policies. These speeches had profound impact on policy making. See Jiang Zemin, "Report on the Forteenth National Congress of the CPC", *People's Daily*, Beijing, 19 October 1992.
10. See Niu (1993), Xu (1993), Young (1993), Sinclair-Loutit (1992), and *Jin Rong Shi Bao* [Financial Times], Beijing, 1 June 1995.
11. Liu. X.D. et al. eds (1994), p. 932.
12. Xiamen Statistics Bureau, *Xiamen Jingji Nianjian* [Economic Almanac of Xiamen], 1994.
13. See Kaye (1992) and Qiao (1994).
14. State Council, *Guowu Yuan Guanyu Shixing Fen Shui Zhi Caizheng Guanli Tizhi de Jueding* [State Council's Resolution On Implementing the Tax Assignment System], Beijing. Ministry of Finance, *Zhongguo Caizheng Nianjian 1994* [Year Book of Chinese Public Finance 1994], Beijing: China Fiscal Press, 1994.
15. *Jingji Ribao* [Economic Daily], Beijing, 3 July 1995; SEZ Research Group (1995).
16. *China Law Brief*, Hong Kong, May, 1995, p. 3.
17. In November 1996, Beijing granted the Suzhou Industrial Park, a Singapore–China joint venture, the same transitional benefits of duty-free imports of machinery or raw material that will be phased out in five years (*Lianhe Zaobao* [United Morning Post] Singapore, 5 December).
18. Guo and Chen (1995).
19. *Business China*, **20** (25), 12 December 1994, pp. 1–2. There are now about 700 open zones at the national and local level, see *Zhong Wai Fangdichan Daobao* [Chinese & Foreign Real Estate Times], Shenzhen, 1995, no. 8, p. 42.
20. For details about these debates, see Wu (1990).
21. *Min Bao*, Hong Kong, 9 August 1995; *Yazhou Zhoukan* [International Chinese News Weekly], 24 September 1995.
22. *The Straits Times*, Singapore, 8 September 1995.
23. *Far Eastern Economic Review*, **158** (45), 9 November 1995, p. 7.
24. Lu, J. (1994).
25. AFP, Reuter, *Straits Times*, Singapore, 2 January 1996.
26. Xinhua News Agency, FE/2586 S1, 15 April 1996.

4. Industry-Oriented Policies

4.1 CENTRALLY PLANNED INDUSTRIALIZATION

The industry-oriented policies reflect China's development strategies and priorities. Compared to industrial policies practised in other developing countries, China's policies have their roots in the tradition of a centrally planned economic system.

The Heavy-Industry Oriented Industrialization

When the People's Republic of China was founded in 1949, rapid industrialization was high on the government's agenda. With a national per capita GNP as low as Rmb 104 by 1952, 90 per cent of the nation's 541-million population lived and worked in the rural areas. Only 10 per cent of the national economy was associated with a modern industrial sector, whereas the rest was in the agricultural and handicraft sectors.[1] Domestically, the CPC government needed to consolidate its rule by lifting the nation from vast poverty through rapid industrialization. Internationally, the government faced the political and economic sanctions of the Western camp. It urgently needed rapid industrialization to develop economic independence and prepare itself for possible military confrontations. Given the support of the then Soviet Union, it was no wonder that China adopted a heavy-industry oriented development strategy in the 1950s. The goal of this strategy was to build the country's capacity to produce capital goods and military supplies as rapidly as possible (for definition of heavy industry and light industry, see Table 4.1).

As in the Soviet Union and other socialist countries at the time, China developed a planning system of short-term (one-year), longer-term (five-year), and even 10- to 20-year perspective plans. The essence of plan formulation was the material balance mechanism, which calculates and balances the main sources of inputs and the main uses of the outputs in the economy.[2] The First Five-Year Plan (1953–1957) set in place the first stage of the heavy-industry oriented rapid industrialization strategy. It aimed at laying down the preliminary foundation for a heavy-industry oriented economic structure. Under the plan, the government mobilized national resources to construct the 156 core heavy-industry projects designed with the help of the Soviet Union and the 694 key construction items. Of the total industrial investment, 85 per cent went to heavy industries.[3]

Table 4.1 Classification of China's Economic Sectors by Agriculture, Light Industry, and Heavy Industries

Sector	Including
1. Agriculture	Farming, forestry, animal husbandry and fishery
2. Light Industry	All industries that produce consumer goods and hand tools
2.1 Light industry sectors using farm products as raw materials	Manufacture of food and beverages, tobacco processing, textile, clothing, fur and leather manufacturing, paper making, etc.
2.2 Light industry sectors using non-farm products as raw materials	Manufacture of cultural and educational articles, crafts and art products, chemical instruments, and manufacture of cultural and office machinery
3. Heavy Industry	All industries that produce capital goods, which provide various sectors of the national economy with necessary materials and a technical base
3.1 Mining and felling industry, which extracts natural resources	Extraction of petroleum, coal, metal and non-metal ores and timber felling
3.2 Raw materials industry, which provides raw materials, fuels and power	Melting and processing of metals, coke making and coke chemistry, chemical materials and building materials, power petroleum and coal processing, etc.
3.3 Manufacturing industry, which processes raw materials	Machine-building industry, industry of metal structure and cement works, industry producing means of agricultural production, and industry of chemical fertilizers and pesticides

Source: *China Statistical Yearbook 1996*, pp. 450–451.

In China's pre-reform economy, the fulfilment of the central plan was implemented by the planned allocation mechanism.[4] The government developed a unified allocation mechanism for all crucial production materials (or capital goods) in the country. According to their relative importance, these materials were classified into three groups and put respectively under the unified allocation of the state, the command of the industrial ministries, and the management of the local governments. Through the state monopoly system for the procurement and sales of agricultural products, the government procured agricultural products at low prices to support the industrialization needs. To provide "cheap" capital for industrialization, the state monobank monopolized the financial sector and suppressed interest rates. Meanwhile the centralized fund-allocation system rationed the limited funds to enterprises according to national production plans. In addition, exports and imports served to fill the resource gaps in the domestic material balance system. To do so the Ministry of International Trade monopolized all foreign trade activities and the state banks centralized foreign exchange administration.

The Self-Reliant Cellular Economy

China's Soviet-style heavy-industry oriented strategy, however, was circumvented by Mao's Utopian economic thoughts. Mao was enthusiastic about building a socialist society that would eradicate the "three basic differences" that caused inequality. These differences were namely the difference that existed between workers and peasants, the one that existed between urban and rural areas, and the one that existed between mental labour and manual labour. To achieve this end, Mao called for organizing self-sufficient communes with very little division of labor and with an egalitarian distribution of income. Mao also rejected the principle of regional specialization and exchange in national economic planning. Instead he favoured regional autonomy and self-reliance. This was partly due to his dislike of a Soviet-type highly centralized state structure and partly due to his worry about a possible open war with the West or the Soviet Union in the 1960s. Mao therefore endorsed a strategy to diffuse and relocate China's industries to the local level and to inland regions.

Based on his views of mass mobilization and regional autonomy, Mao advocated a policy of "walking on two legs". According to this policy, the rural development of local small industries based on simple technology should go in parallel with the development of large and medium-sized modern plants in urban areas. All provinces were encouraged to build themselves small but comprehensive industrial systems. These systems should be fairly self-sufficient in the production of raw materials, machinery and consumer goods.

National and regional self-reliance was the core idea of the Maoist economic strategy. Such a strategy rested on the human willpower which Mao believed could break the routine of economic development and create miracles. He claimed that China need not trail behind other countries, following their "beaten path" in achieving economic development.[5]

Under Mao's influence, two political campaigns, namely the "Great Leap Forward Movement" (1958–60) and the "Great Proletarian Cultural Revolution" (1966–76), caused harsh interruptions to the centrally planned industrialization process. During the Great Leap Forward Movement, the CPC resorted to exhaustive mass mobilization in a vain attempt to reach unrealistic output targets for iron and steel production and grain production. Under political pressures, the planning administration had repeatedly to revise the Second Five-Year Plan (1958–62) to meet the Party leaders' ambitious demands for high-speed growth. The Great Leap Forward caused great waste of resources and eventually led to disastrous results to the economy. As a consequence, the government had to spend three years (1963–65) on "economic retrenchment" to repair the damages.

The fulfilment of the Third Five-Year Plan (1966–70) was interrupted and undermined by the Cultural Revolution, during which thousands of government officials were purged. The planning apparatus incurred severe damage in the peak years of the Cultural Revolution. National economic planning was virtually suspended in 1967–68. Mao's thoughts also profoundly affected the working of the Fourth Five-Year Plan (1971–75). National economic development was all geared up to prepare the country for a possible full-scale war against foreign invasion. All provinces and regions were encouraged to develop their "comprehensive and independent" economies. A major consequence was the development of the so-called "cellular economy", which consisted of small, self-sufficient units operating at the regional level.[6]

Legacies of Mao

Nevertheless, the heavy-industry development strategy was not inconsistent with Mao's thoughts. It worked through the Mao Era and turned China from an agricultural economy to a self-sufficient semi-industrialized power armed with nuclear war facilities. As shown in Table A2.3, except for the retrenchment period of 1963–65, heavy industry grew much faster than light industry and agriculture. Although China achieved rather high rates of economic growth in the pre-reform period (1952–1978), there is evidence that the growth was very inefficient. Centrally planned resource allocation imposed an unusually high level of savings on the population and made people forego their current consumption for capital investment. This resulted in a very high rate of accumulation in the Mao Era (Table A2.3).

The high rate of accumulation, however, failed to generate efficient growth. Chow (1993) used annual data from 1952–80 to estimate production functions for China's aggregate economy and for the five sectors – agriculture, industry, construction, transportation and commerce. He found that capital formation was the main source of growth and technological progress was absent in the growth during the period. A World Bank study also found that, for the production of one unit of gross domestic product in the early 1980s, China's consumption of energy, steel and transportation was 12 to 560 per cent higher than that in India, South Korea and Brazil. China's total factor productivity between 1957 and 1982 was in a state of stagnation or even negative growth.[7] Lin et al. (1996) argued that giving development priority to heavy industry, which is capital intensive and of long-term investment, undermined China's comparative advantages in abundant labour resources. The government's defence-oriented investment strategy to diffuse and relocate industrial projects into China's inland mountainous areas had also contributed to high costs of capital construction.[8] During the period of the First Five-Year Plan, every Rmb 100 of such investment used to generate Rmb 83.6 of fixed assets in projects completed and put into use. In the period 1967-76, however, the figure dropped to Rmb 59.6. The ratio between the increased national income and national accumulation had declined. It was 35 per cent for the First Five-Year Plan period but dropped to 26 per cent and 16 per cent respectively for the periods of the Third and Fourth Five-Year Plans.[9]

Striving for the "Four Modernizations"

The period of the Fifth Five-Year Plan (1976–80) was a turning point in China's economic development. Led by the then Party head, Hua Guofeng, the Eleventh National Congress of the CPC held in August 1977 called for the achievement of the "four modernizations" by the end of the century. These "modernizations" refer to modernization in agriculture, modernization in industry, modernization in science and technology, and modernization in national defence.

During 1977–78, the Chinese government proposed an ambitious ten-year programme to modernize China's economy (see Table A2.1 in Appendix 2). To fulfil the programme, the state increased investment in capital construction from 1977's Rmb 31.2 billion to 1978's 41.7 billion, a sharp rise of 33.7 per cent. It was planned to increase the investment by another 15.7 per cent in 1979. The government continued to carry out a mainly heavy-industry oriented development strategy. Accordingly, the rate of accumulation (the proportion of national income that is not used for current year consumption) rose from 32.3 per cent in 1977 to 36.5 per cent in 1978.

This caused great tension in an already difficult economic situation. The government budget deficit soared. Imports of grains, steel and other raw materials increased sharply and about one quarter of the enterprises could not operate normally due to severe shortages of energy.[10] The economic woes eventually led to the change of the Party's leadership and policy at the landmark Third Plenary of the Eleventh CPC Central Committee in December 1978. At the Plenary, the Party decided to spend at least two years on an economic adjustment and retrenchment programme.

4.2 THE NEW LONG MARCH

The leadership change in December 1978 marked the commencement of China's market-oriented reform and a fundamental change in national development strategy. From 1979 to 1981, the economic retrenchment reduced budget deficit and cut the state's investment in capital construction. Consequently the accumulation rate fell to 28.5 per cent in 1981. Meanwhile the Party leadership critically reviewed its past economic strategies and vowed to abandon the inefficient development plans. In a report to the National People's Congress, Zhao Ziyang, the then Premier, pointed out that, during 1952–80, China increased her industrial capital assets 26 times and gross product value 8.1 times. In the same period, however, national income increased only 4.2 times and per capita consumption only doubled. To rectify the inefficient growth pattern, he suggested a 10-point guideline for future economic development, which stressed the promotion of economic efficiency.[11]

Quadrupling Output Values in 20 Years

At the Twelfth National Congress of the CPC held in September 1982, the Party proposed a 20-year long-term development goal and called for "a new long march" to fulfil the goal.[12] According to this plan, from 1981 to 2000, China would quadruple her annual gross value of industry and agriculture with increasing efficiency. To achieve this goal, three areas would become the "strategic foci". One area was agriculture. The second was energy and transportation and the third was education and science. The 20-year development was to consist of two periods. The first decade was a period to accumulate capacity and lay a solid ground for economic booms in the second period (1991–2000). Economic reform was instrumental to raise efficiency and restructure the economy for further growth.[13]

The Sixth Five-Year Plan (1981–85) and the Seventh Five-Year Plan (1986–90) covered the first period of the 20-year plan. Both plans specified the quantitative objectives of overall national economic performance as well as growth targets for major sectors. They also presented targets of changes in industrial structures (see Table 4.2 for the classification of industries).

Table 4.2 Industrial Classification According to Historical Sequence of Development (introduced in mid-1980s)

Industry	Including
1. Primary Industry: agriculture	Farming, forestry, animal husbandry, and fishery
2. Secondary Industry: industry	Extraction; manufacturing; electric power, gas, and water production and supply; and construction
3. Tertiary Industry: all other industries	
3.1 The first level (circulation sector)	Transportation, post and telecommunications services; Wholesale, retail trade, and food services
3.2 The second level (service sector providing service for production and consumption)	Banking and insurance; geological prospecting and water conservancy; real estate; social services; scientific research and polytechnic services
3.3 The third level (service for improving education, health and cultural life)	Health care, sports and social welfare; education, culture, art, radio, film and television
3.4 The fourth level (service for public needs)	Government agencies, party agencies and social organizations

Source: *China Statistical Yearbook 1996*, pp. 63–64.

For instance, the Sixth Five-Year Plan spelt out that capital construction investment should be focused on energy supply and transportation sectors. Adjustment of heavy industry's product structure and service orientation was also on the agenda. The industrial policy was more pronounced in the Seventh Five-Year Plan, which emphasized development of energy and raw material industries, transportation and telecommunications industries, and the construction sector. It also promoted the growth of the tertiary industry and several new industrial sectors.[14] The Plan was the first one in China's planning history that set percentage targets for industrial structures (see Table A2.4). It was also the first five-year plan that pledged to switch the construction focus onto the technological upgrading of existing enterprises. With regard to foreign trade, the Plan required a gradual increase of the share of manufactured products in exports.

Central Planning with Fewer Commands

The nature of economic planning changed drastically during the decade. As discussed in Sections 1.2 and 2.1, economic reform in the 1980s marketized and monetarized China's economy. Investment, production and consumption became more market-oriented. Direct state control of resource allocation was on the wane thanks to the following reforms.

First, through the 1980s, there was an across-the-board reduction in the types, quantities and scope of material allocated by the unified state plan. In the early 1980s, state enterprises were allowed to sell their products after meeting the state plans. Some plan-allocated goods were made available for orders by enterprises. Production material markets were set up to facilitate resource mobility. Starting from 1984, the state took measures to gradually liberalize outside-plan prices and adjust planned prices. While the state plans still guaranteed material supplies for important production activities and key construction projects after 1985, the quantity of such planned material supply was kept at the 1984 level. From 1980 to 1988, the number of materials in the state unified plan decreased from 256 to 27, the number of materials under ministry-level instructive plans was cut from 316 to 45. By the late 1980s, majority of the plan-allocated materials were eventually traded in market.

Second, the government introduced into the rural area the household responsibility based on output quota. By doing so, the state resumed an in-kind agricultural tax system. The state monopoly for the procurement and sales of agricultural products was therefore phased out in the 1980s.

Third, for state enterprises, two major reform schemes were introduced in 1983 and 1984 to set up a corporate tax system that would allow substantial retained earnings at the firm level. One was the so-called "*li gai shui*" (taxes-for-profits), which sought to dismantle the system where all profits after subtracting a small retained portion for the enterprise were simply returned to the state. By 1986, almost all enterprise profits were taxed, instead of being remitted to the government. Another was the so-called "*bo gai dai*" (loans-for-grants). The reform strove to move away from the provision of investment funds on a grant basis from the government budget toward the allocation of working capital and investment funds through the banking system. Accordingly, the government gradually reduced the number of products included in the state's instructive plan from 120 in 1979 to 58 in 1990. The share of these products in the total value of industrial products dropped from 40 per cent to 16 per cent.

Fourth, with the loans-for-grants reform, the People's Bank of China was restructured into a central bank in 1984. Meanwhile four big state-owned "specialized banks" were reorganised or established to take over regular banking business in the period 1979–84. These banks include the Bank of China (BOC, 1979), the Agricultural Bank of China (ABC, 1979), the People's Construction Bank (PCB, 1981), and the Industrial & Commercial Bank of China (ICBC, 1984). The goal was to develop these specialized banks into full-fledged commercial banks. Since the landmark restructure of the Bank of Communications (BOCOM) into a quasi-commercial bank in 1986, there have emerged a few more smaller-sized commercial banks and many non-bank financial institutions, which are organized on a share-holding basis.

Fifth, the fiscal system was no longer a centralized one. Fiscal reforms changed the previously highly centralized budget system to a system featuring stratified management with revenue-sharing at local levels. In the 1980s, the central government signed revenue sharing contracts with provincial and local governments that fixed an annual lump-sum payment to the central government for a period of several years. After meeting the payment quota, the local government would retain the rest. Under this framework, the local governments greatly increased their decision-making power over the uses of budget revenues.

Table 4.3 *Sources of Investment in Fixed Assets (percentage)*

Source	1980	1985	1990	1995
State appropriation	44.7	16.0	8.7	3.1
Domestic loans	11.7	20.1	19.6	21.0
Foreign investment	7.2	3.6	6.3	11.5
Fundraising	N/A	N/A	52.4	53.2
Others	36.5	60.3	13.1	13.8

Note: The figures in "others" for 1980 and 1985 include the figures for "fundraising".

Source: *Statistical Yearbook of China's Economy* 1992 and 1996, p. 24 and p. 139, respectively.

Finally, the open-door policy transformed the Chinese economy from a near autarky to an active participant in the world economy. From 1979 to 1990, as the state gave up its monopoly over foreign trade, the number of exported goods handled by the state decreased from 900 to 27. The share of exports in GDP rose from less than 5 per cent in 1978 to more than 20 per cent in the early 1990s.

Thanks to the above reforms in the 1980s, there occurred fundamental changes in the way that investment in fixed capital was financed. Table 4.3 shows these changes.

The Teeth That Can Still Bite

Despite the waning direct controls by the state, the Sixth Five-Year Plan (1981–85) and the Seventh Five-Year Plan (1986–90) were not "toothless" plans. They actually worked much more successfully than earlier plans (see Tables A2.4 and A2.5). There remained several instruments to carry out national plans.

First, after 1984, the state still controlled the usage of major capital resources through the credit quota plans of the state banking system. Credit quota plans allocated financial resources among regions and industries. From 1985, all state investment funds for capital construction have been appropriated through bank loans. The state specialized banks are obliged to provide the so-called "policy-related loans" to meet the priorities set by the government. By 1994, such policy loans accounted for 40 per cent of the loans lent by the four major specialized banks. For example, the Industrial & Commercial Bank of China is responsible for supporting the circular fund needs and technology-upgrading needs of some large state-owned firms. The Agricultural Bank of China must provide loans to meet the needs for procurement and warehousing of certain important agricultural products. Loans by the People's Construction Bank go first to national priority projects and firms. The Bank of China should support the fulfilment of centrally planned export and import items.

Second, for years, the official interest rates have been below the market clearing level. Some policy loans, such as those for capital investment in agriculture and infrastructure development and those for circular-fund needs in grain procurement, have enjoyed preferential interest rates, which are even lower than the standard rates. The state banks' interest rate policy has been structured along the government's industry-oriented and region-oriented policies. For instance, the annual interest rate of loans for capital construction varied from 2.4 per cent to 12 per cent, depending on industries, regions, and projects.[15]

Third, the state has retained the approval power for large capital construction projects. The Sixth Five-Year Plan specified that all large and medium-sized capital construction projects must get approval from the State Planning Commission. The small projects should go through the province-level planning commissions and the state council. The approval authorities have changed over the years but the stratified administrative system of project approval remains for investment in capital construction. For foreign investment, the MOFTEC has granted limited powers to approve equity joint ventures and wholly foreign-owned enterprises to province-level governments and a number of cities. Similar to provincial governments, some important ministries, such as the Ministries of Metallurgical Industry, Water Resources, Energy and Agriculture, also have the province-level power to approve investment projects. The ministry-level approval power varies as a reflection of China's industrial policy (see Table 3.2 for details).

Table 4.4 Taxes on Investment (For Indigenous Enterprises Only)

Tax or Levy (year started)	Payer	Tax Base	Rate	Features
Construction tax (1983)	State-owned enterprises, urban collective enterprises, government and army units	capital construction not funded by state budget	10% of the investment project value (exempted for energy, transportation and education-health projects)	To control extra-budgetary capital construction
Adjusted construction tax (1987)	same as above	same as above	10% for most projects, 20% and 30% for hotels, restaurants, and office buildings	To control extra-budgetary projects and guide investment direction
Coordinating tax for the directions of fixed capital investment (1991)	All units or individuals who invest in fixed capital construction	Capital construction investment and upgrading/ renovation investment	Five rates from 0% to 30% according to investment contents	To carry out industrial policies

Source: Xu and Yu eds (1994), pp. 239–245; Zhang and Wu eds (1994), pp. 392–410.

Table 4.5 Taxes and Levies to Support Certain Industries or Sectors (For Indigenous Enterprises Only)

Tax or Levy (year started)	Payer	Tax Base	Rate	Features
Resource tax (1984)	Enterprises or individuals who extract petroleum, coal, gas and iron ore	Physical output units	Vary according to resource qualities	To generate revenue for resource protection
Urban maintenance and construction tax (1985)	Enterprises or individuals who pay product tax, value-added tax, or operation tax	Product tax, value-added tax or operation tax	5–7% on any of the three taxes payable	To finance urban maintenance and construction
Energy and transportation construction levy (1983)	State-owned enterprises, urban collective enterprises, government and army units	after-tax profits	10%	To fund energy and transportation construction
Education fees (1986)	State-owned enterprises, urban collective enterprises, government and army units	Product tax, value-added tax or operation tax	1% on any of the three taxes payable (2% after 1990)	To finance local education

Source: Zhang and Wu eds (1994), pp. 60–86; Xu and Yu eds (1994), pp. 3–44; Zhao ed (1989), pp. 667–673.

Fourth, although the state reduced the types, quantities and scope of materials allocated by the unified state plan, it still retained the control of some crucial materials under the two-track pricing system in the 1980s. The state still controls the prices of fuel and energy supplies, railroad transportation and telecommunications. State monopolies continues to dominate these sectors.

Fifth, taxation and levies have been important instruments in carrying out state plans. In the "taxes-for-profits" reform, Beijing introduced major basic taxes with various rates, which reflected planned priorities. On top of those taxes, there were a number of taxes and levies aiming to promote desired industrial structures and implement macroeconomic policies. Up to 1994, there were 37 taxes with six major categories, namely turnover taxes, income taxes, resource taxes, property taxes, behaviour taxes, and taxes for foreign firms and individuals. Tables 4.4, 4.5 and 4.6 list the major taxes that had clear signs of state plans for inter-industrial resource allocation.

Table 4.6 Turnover Taxes Before 1994 (For Indigenous Enterprises Only)

Tax or Levy (year started)	Payer	Tax Base	Rate	Features
Product tax (1950)	Enterprises or individuals who produce or import products	Sales	22 rates vary from 3% to 60% with 24 categories and 260 items for industrial products	Rates vary for different industries and product items
Value-added tax (1980–84)	Enterprises or individuals who add values to products	Added values	12 rates vary from 8% to 45% with 31 major items	Rates vary for different product items
Business tax (1950)	Commerce and service enterprises	Sales	5 rates vary from 3% to 15% with 14 items	Rates vary for different service items

Source: Zhang and Wu eds (1994), pp. 60–86; Xu and Yu eds (1994), pp. 3–44.

Sixth, when production or investment involves use and exchange of foreign currencies, the state bank's control of foreign exchanges could play a pivotal role. Even in the case where local governments and trading companies legally retain their share of foreign exchange earnings, the state still can intervene when it considers necessary.

Seventh, through state trading companies, the government can implement its priorities in export and import activities. The government can also ban or encourage certain exports or imports by issuing administrative directives and/or imposing tariff or non-tariff barriers.

Finally, when the government sees the need to restructure an industry, it can persuade and even direct the state-owned enterprises in question to merge, form business groups, or regroup themselves. This measure has been frequently used in recent years as a scheme to rescue the state-owned enterprises in troubles.

Successful Implementation or Poor Forecasts

From Table A2.4, one can observe that China did pretty well in achieving the economic growth targets during the Sixth Five-Year Plan period. All growth targets (except for exports) were well surpassed by at least four percentage points. It is specially noteworthy that the per capita consumption increased at an annual rate of 9.6 per cent, indicating rapidly rising living standards.

These overwhelming successes, however, could imply that the Plan was too conservative to provide meaningful guidance for the real progress. Given the sweeping institutional changes in the early 1980s, this "failure" was nevertheless understandable.

The real economic performance not only upset the Plan's forecasts of most growth rates but also disregarded the industrial structure goals defined by the Plan. For instance, the efforts to adjust the percentage output ratios of agriculture, light industry and heavy industry did not produce the desired results. The ratio in 1985 was almost the same as that in 1980 (27.2:34.3:38.5).

The target of keeping the accumulation rate below 30 per cent of national income was also missed. By percentage, the investment in energy supply sector fell below the planned target although the absolute value had surpassed the planned one. As for the efficiency target, China again failed to reach the planned target of reducing consumption of energy per Rmb 10,000 of national income down to 7.15 tons by 1990. Contrarily, the consumption level increased from 1980's 8.15 tons to 1985's 8.43 tons.

Compared with the Sixth Plan, the Seventh Five-Year Plan was a better forecast for most growth targets. Most growth targets were surpassed with comfortable margins (Table A2.5).

The economy also hit the planned targets for industrial structures more punctually. In terms of investment in capital construction and the accumulation rate, the implementation of the Seventh Plan was again more effective. In particular, the government successfully increased the capital construction investment in the energy supply sector, laying down a good foundation for further economic growth in the 1990s.

Equally successful achievement was the increase of energy use efficiency, which lowered the energy consumption per Rmb 10,000 of national income well below the planned level. It was nevertheless a pity that the remarkable economic growth failed to raise the per capita consumption fast enough to meet the planned requirement.

In foreign trade, the manufactured goods accounted for no more than 50 per cent of China's export value during the first half of the 1980s. During the Seventh Five-Year Plan, however, China significantly increased her international competitiveness in manufactured exports. While the nominal value of exports grew at an annual rate of over 17 per cent, the proportion of manufactured goods in total export value rose to 74.5 per cent.

4.3 THE ERA OF INDUSTRIAL POLICY

By the late 1980s, after a decade of economic reform and opening up, the Chinese economy had made great progress. In the 1980s China's total industrial output value increased 2.3 times while her total agricultural output value increased 84.6 per cent. The total value of investment in fixed assets in the 1980s reached Rmb 2,770 billion, more than the total investment made during 1950–1980.[16]

The continuous economic boom, accompanied by the worsening status of the state budget, however, led to a new fear of hyperinflation when an overall price liberalization programme was put on the agenda in 1988. Amidst a nation-wide wave of panic purchases, bank runs and price hikes, the government decided to slow down the pace of reform and implement a retrenchment programme to cool the overheating economy.

The First Explicit National Industrial Policy

At this juncture, China's policy-makers also reflected the country's long-term development strategies. In March 1989, the State Council issued the "Decision on the Gist of Current Industrial Policy", the first explicit and detailed official guideline for a national industrial policy.[17]

The document perceived that there existed four serious problems in China's industrial structure. First, the production capacity of the manufacturing industries was too big for the relatively underdeveloped agricultural sector, energy and raw material industries, and transportation sector. Second, the production capacity of average-level manufacturing industries was too big and the capacity of advanced-level manufacturing was in shortage. Third, inter-regional distribution of industries was not rational and regional (comparative) advantages were not utilized. Fourth, inter-enterprise organization, coordination and linkage were not well organized. Industrial concentration was too low to be efficient.

Industrial policy refers to government attempts to channel resources into sectors that it views as important for future economic growth. The "Decision" put forward the major principles of China's industrial policy. These include:

- Guiding market development, coordinating aggregate demand and aggregate supply, reducing inconsistency between the consumption structure and industrial structure;
- Reducing and suppressing production and investment in goods in excess supply, increasing and expanding production and investment in those in shortage. Concentrating on the production of grain, cotton, coal,

electricity power supply, transportation, and other light industrial products in shortage;

- Decisions on priorities and constraints should be based on the consideration of market demand, industrial linkage, technology progress, capacity to earn foreign exchanges, and economic efficiency.

According to the above principles, the document gave a list of industries and products that should receive priorities, including:

1. Agriculture and agriculture-service industries;
2. Some products in light industry and textile industry;
3. Infrastructure and basic industries, such as transportation of coal, agricultural input, and passengers, telecommunications, energy supplies (coal, electricity and petroleum), some important raw materials (iron, non-ferrous metal, chemicals);
4. Machinery and electronic industries, especially high value-added products;
5. High-tech industries, including areospace products, new materials, and bioengineering technology;
6. Exports that earn good profits and foreign exchanges, especially manufacturing goods.

The document also defined the areas of production to be suppressed and constrained. These mainly included low quality products and machinery, consumer durable goods that were "luxury" in electricity consumption, "luxury" consumer products that needed production inputs in shortage, production modes that were obsolete, energy wasting and environment polluting. There was also a list of products or production activities to be banned.

In consistency with the priority industries and products, the document also listed the areas where the state would support investment in capital construction and technology upgrading. In areas subject to suppression and bans, investment would be strictly controlled. On top of that, the Decision specified that exports of high value-added manufacturing goods and domestically abundant commodities should be encouraged. Strict plans should apply to the export of major resource commodities, which are vital to national interests. Export of goods in severe shortage in the domestic economy should be banned.

As for the measures to ensure the implementation of these policies, they were not much different from the planning instruments we discussed in the previous section. In particular, the document emphasized the importance of setting priorities for bank loans and using differential tax rates to guide industrial development. What is noteworthy is the application of these industrial policies to guide foreign investors. Since the promulgation of the Decision, the MOFTEC has made systematic efforts through the guideline to influence the direction and structure of foreign direct investment. It has published lists of sectors and product categories where investment should be actively encouraged. Favourable approval procedures, tax concessions, cooperation from the state-owned enterprises, and other incentives have been provided at central and local levels to support those preferred investments.

A More Industry-Oriented Five-Year Plan

In April 1991, the National People's Congress approved the Eighth Five-Plan (1991–95) and the Ten-Year Plan for National Economic and Social Development (1991–2000). Both of these two plans regarded the adjustment of industrial structures as the foremost development goal.

The Ten-Year Plan called for efforts to strengthen agriculture, basic industries and infrastructure facilities. It vowed to restructure and upgrade the manufacturing industry. The Plan gave priority to the development of the electronic industry and urged an active promotion for the construction sector and tertiary industry (see Table A2.1).

Accordingly, the Eighth Five-Year Plan (1991–95) stressed the development of 12 sectors and specified output and construction targets for them. These sectors include: agriculture and rural economy, irrigation and water conservancy, energy industry, transportation and telecommunications, raw material industry, geological prospecting and weather forecasting, electronic industry, advanced machinery industry, defence industry and research, certain products in light and textile industries, construction sector, and certain commercial services.

In regard to foreign trade, the Plan took a step further from the Seventh Plan to promote the exports of manufactured goods, in particular the machinery products, electrical equipment, light industry products and textile products, and high-tech products. The Plan pledged to increase export quality and adjust the export structure toward one more reliant on higher value-added manufactured goods.

Planning Capital Flows

Compared to the two five-year plans in the 1980s, this plan did not give a target composition of fixed capital investment but spelled out more detailed plans for further economic reforms.[18] This change might be due to the fact that the proportion of fixed capital investment under direct state control had declined over the years and more attention was paid to other measures to influence investment activities (see Table 4.3). The Plan nevertheless demanded measures to direct the flow of foreign direct investment in line with the state industrial policies.

Table 4.7 Capital Construction Investment of State-Owned Units by Sector (in Rmb billion)

Sector	Seventh FYP	Eighth FYP	Increased by
Agriculture, forestry, husbandry and fishery	10.45 (1.42%)	25.66 (1.09%)	145%
Extraction	76.73 (10.44%)	173.02 (7.34%)	125%
Electricity, gas, water supply	133.90 (18.22%)	415.96 (17.64%)	211%
Construction	7.34 (1.00%)	43.49 (1.84%)	493%
Geological prospecting and water conservancy	16.70 (2.27%)	52.56 (2.23%)	215%
Transportation, storage, postal and telecommunications services	98.10 (13.35%)	465.94 (19.76%)	375%
Total	734.90	2358.50	221%

Note: The percentage figure in brackets refers to the proportion of the investment in that category to the total capital construction investment of the year.

Source: *China Statistical Yearbook 1996*, pp. 148–149.

Table 4.7 displays the amounts and shares of capital construction investment in several sectors that were supposed to receive priority according to the Eighth Five-Year Plan. Compared to that in the period 1986–90, the investment in all these sectors was more than doubled in the period 1991–95.

It is noteworthy, however, only the categories "construction" and "transportation, storage, postal and telecommunications service sectors" saw their weights in the total capital construction investment increased. The main cause of this inconsistency between the planned priority and the reality could be the across-the-board overshooting of the state-owned units' investment quota during the period. The amount of capital construction investment planned for these units in the five-year period was Rmb 840 billion while the money actually invested exceeded Rmb 2,300 billion.

Industry-Oriented Tax Policies

Preferential tax policy has served as another important support for the priority sectors. In the early 1990s, the government offered first-year exemption and second-year half rate for corporate income taxes for newly opened enterprises in transportation and postal and telecommunications service sectors. Foreign-funded enterprises engaged in businesses of energy industry, transportation sectors and infrastructure could enjoy corporate income tax exemptions and reductions (see Tables A1.3 and A1.4).

In 1994, China launched a comprehensive tax reform to unify all enterprises' corporate income taxes to a flat rate of 33 per cent. The central government, however, announced in March 1994 that it would grant income tax exemptions and concessions to certain businesses:

1. The high-tech enterprises in High-Tech Industrial Development Zones may get a 15-per cent reduction of their income tax. The new high-tech enterprises in these zones may be exempt from paying income tax for two years after they start operation;
2. Most new businesses in the tertiary industry can be granted income tax exemption or reduction for one to two years. These include new firms engaging in consulting services, transportation or telecommunications services, public utilities, health, storage, tourism, foreign trade, commerce, catering, home service, education, culture, etc. The firms providing agricultural service and institutes or colleges doing technological training and technology transfer, consulting and service, may be exempt from paying income tax;
3. Firms in production using recycled materials may be exempt from income tax for five years;
4. Incomes from technology transfer with annual income no more than Rmb 300,000 may be exempt from tax;
5. Educational institutions' workshops, enterprises specially set up for handicapped persons, and service enterprises specially set up for hiring urban unemployed persons may get income tax exemption or reduction;
6. Township and village enterprises may pay reduced income tax by 10 per cent for community expenses;
7. New enterprises in some impoverished areas may get tax exemption or reduction for three years.

Most of the above income tax benefits (1–4) are industry-oriented. The others mainly work for social welfare purposes.

An important tax policy has been the coordinating tax for directions of fixed capital investment, which was introduced in 1991 to be levied on indigenous enterprises (see Table 4.4). A zero tax rate applies to projects "urgently needed by the state". These projects include fixed capital investment in agriculture and water conservancy, energy industry, transportation, postal and telecommunications, some important raw materials industries, geological prospecting, certain medical projects, certain electronic and machinery projects, pollution control, urban public utilities, some storage facilities, etc. For those projects encouraged by the state but constrained by energy supply and transportation facilities, the low 5 per cent tax rate applies. For those projects that are of inefficient scale, outmoded technologies or products already in excess supply, the state policy is to strictly control their development and therefore the highest rate of 30 per cent is applied.[19] All the other projects should be taxed at a rate of 15 per cent.[20]

Table 4.8 displays the industrial variance in burdens of sales-related taxes. The extraction and raw material sector's effective tax rate was the highest in 1990 and 1995. This could be due to the effect of the resource tax (see Table 4.6) imposed on the extraction industry. In 1990, the rate for the extraction and raw material sector was 26.5 per cent higher than the heavy industry average. In 1995, it was only 22.5 per cent higher, indicating a lower tax burden.

Table 4.8 Burdens of Sales-Related Taxes of Industrial Enterprises by Sectors (Unit: Rmb billions)

1990	Pre-tax Profit	After-tax Profit	Sales-related Tax	Effective Rate
Heavy industry	102.891	34.684	68.207	7.59%
Of which: Manufacturing	38.247	17.517	20.73	5.13%
Extraction and raw materials	64.64	17.17	47.477	9.60%
Selected manufacturing sectors				
Special purpose equipment manufacturing	3.195	1.557	1.638	5.44%
Electronic and telecommunications	4.255	2.294	1.961	3.77%
Instruments, meters, cultural and official machinery	1.166	0.592	0.574	5.69%
National total	194.588	55.981	138.607	8.25%

Table 4.8 Continued

1995	Pretax Profit	Post-tax Profit	Sales Tax	Effective Rate
Heavy industry	313.26	112.98	200.285	6.48%
Of which:				
Manufacturing	110.94	42.60	68.34	4.79%
Extraction and raw materials	202.33	70.38	131.95	7.94%
Extraction	52.29	20.03	32.26	9.68%
Raw materials	150.04	50.35	99.69	7.50%
Selected manufacturings sectors				
Special purpose equipment manufacturing	10.16	2.69	7.471	4.55%
Electronic and telecommunications	18.50	11.68	6.819	2.81%
Instruments, meters, cultural and official machinery	2.62	0.69	1.927	4.62%
National total	505.03	163.49	341.54	6.45%

Source: *China Statistical Yearbook 1990*, pp. 399–401, *China Statistical Yearbook 1995*, pp. 414–417.

All the three selected sectors, which received priorities in the Eighth Five-Year Plan, enjoyed lower-than-average effective tax rates in the heavy industry and the national economy. The electronic and telecommunications manufacturing had the most preferential tax rates for both years. The other two selected sectors saw their tax rates fall from above-average levels in the manufacturing industry to lower-than-average levels in these five years. Meanwhile, heavy industry in 1990 had a more preferential tax rate compared to the whole industry sector but lost the benefit in 1995.

The "Best Fulfilled Plan"

The Fourth Session of the Eighth National People's Congress held in March 1996 hailed the Eighth Five-Year Plan one of "the best fulfilled five-year plans" ever the founding of the PRC. By 1995, China had fulfilled the target of quadrupling GNP over the level of the year 1980 (calculated at comparable prices) five years ahead of the agenda set by the Ten-Year Plan for National Economic and Social Development (1991–2000).

From any perspective, 1991–1995 was a period of hyper-economic growth (see Table A2.6). The speedy economic growth was accompanied by a rapid growth of per capita resident consumption at an annual rate of 10.7 per cent. What is remarkable is that for the first time since 1980 the target of energy efficiency was reached.

Hand-Picking Winners: Partial Success

The industrial policies stated in the Eighth Five-Year Plan, however, had only been partially successful in changing China's industrial structure. From Table 4.9, we observe that the share of the primary sector in domestic production had declined steadily over the years, reflecting China's industrialization process. The share of the construction sector dipped to 4.12 per cent in 1990 but rose sharply to 4.49 per cent in 1995. The two supposedly prioritized categories, namely "transportation, postal and telecommunications services" and "other tertiary sectors", saw their shares rise in the late 1980s but the trend was reversed in the first half of the 1990s.

Table 4.9 Change of GDP Composition by Sector

Sectors	1980	1985	1990	1995
Primary	30.09%	26.88%	22.58%	15.10%
Industry	44.19%	42.60%	45.31%	55.95%
Construction	4.33%	4.40%	4.12%	4.49%
Transportation, postal and telecommunications services	4.54%	4.46%	4.88%	4.41%
Commerce	4.73%	7.33%	6.28%	5.08%
Other tertiary sectors	12.13%	14.34%	16.83%	14.97%
Total	100.00%	100.00%	100.00%	100.00%

Source: China Statistical Yearbook 1996, p. 42.

When we turn to structural changes within the industrial sector, we find that heavy industry grew faster than the national industrial sector in terms of both output value and sales. In terms of fixed asset value increase, the heavy industry grew at about the same speed as the national industry (Table 4.10).

Within heavy industry, the growth of the extraction and raw material sectors lagged behind the growth of the manufacturing sector in terms of output, sales and fixed assets (Table 4.10). This result does not appear to have met the priorities put forward in the Five-Year Plan. In the manufacturing sector, all the three prioritized sub-sectors were outstanding in growth of output, asset value and sales.

Table 4.10(I) *Change of Gross Industrial Output Value by Industrial Sector*

Sector	1990	1995	Change
Heavy industry	991.25	3,145.62	217%
Of which:			
Manufacturing	459.00	1,518.87	231%
Extraction and raw materials	532.25	1,626.75	206%
Selected manufacturing sectors			
Special purpose equipment manufacturing	34.13	175.65	415%
Electronic and telecommunications	58.42	253.05	333%
Instruments, meters, cultural and official machinery	11.01	42.57	287%
National total	1,868.92	5,494.69	194%

Source: *China Statistical Yearbook 1991* and *1996.*

Table 4.10 (II) *Change of Fixed Assets by Industrial Sector*

Sector	1990	1995	Change
Heavy industry	712.94	2,664.82	274%
Of which:			
Manufacturing	210.22	874.94	316%
Extraction and raw materials	502.72	1,789.87	256%
Selected manufacturing sectors			
Special purpose equipment manufacturing	17.54	99.15	465%
Electronic and telecommunications	18.10	94.27	421%
Instruments, meters, cultural and official machinery	5.66	24.64	335%
National total	1,016.89	3,844.43	278%

Source: *China Statistical Yearbook 1991* and *1996.*

The growth patterns of all these sectors were generally consistent with the unequal tax burdens they had borne (Table 4.8). The three manufacturing sub-sectors apparently benefited from the preferential tax treatments they received during the period while the extraction and raw materials sectors might have been retarded by their heavier tax burdens.

Table 4.10 (III) Change of Sales by Industrial Sector

Sector	1990	1995	Change
Heavy industry	898.313	3,089.82	244%
Of which:			
Manufacturing	403.95	1,427.27	253%
Extraction and raw materials	494.37	1,662.55	236%
Selected manufacturing sectors			
Special purpose equipment manufacturing	10.08	164.33	446%
Electronic and telecommunications	52.07	242.46	366%
Instruments, meters, cultural and official machinery	10.08	41.67	313%
National total	1,679.31	5,293.62	215%

Note: All figures are current year values

Source: *China Statistical Yearbook 1991* and *1996*.

In the area of foreign trade, China had remarkable success in implementing the planned adjustment of export structure. During the Eighth Five-Year Plan period, the proportion of manufactured goods in total export value rose from 74.5 per cent to 85.6 per cent. In particular, the share of machinery and transportation equipment in total export value increased from 11.5 per cent to 21.1 per cent.

4.4 GUIDED INVESTMENT

The taste of the first national industrial policy of 1989 during the first half of the 1990s had prompted Chinese planners to develop a more comprehensive and operational industrial policy system. Before China concluded her Eighth Five-Year Plan, the State Council promulgated "The Outline of State Industrial Policy in the 1990s" in June 1994.[21]

Ambitions and Steps

The "Outline" specified the main direction and aspects of China's industrial restructuring during the 1990s as follows:

- Continuously strengthening the status of agriculture as the foundation of the national economy, developing the rural economy in an all-round way;
- Vigorously beefing up basic industries, striving to relieve the strain posed by the slow development of basic industries and infrastructure;
- Accelerating the development of mainstay (pillar) industries to promote overall national economic development. These industries include the machinery industry, electronic industry, petroleum processing and raw chemical materials industry, automobile industry, and construction industry;
- Rationally restructuring foreign trade, sharpening the competitive edge of the national industries in the world market. The foreign trade policy should encourage exports of agricultural products with comparative advantages, home electronic appliances, products of high added-value and international competitiveness, products of new and high technologies. Encouragement was also granted to imports of crucial parts, equipment and technologies. Exports of primary goods and energy intensive goods would, however, be gradually reduced or restricted. Imports of luxurious consumer goods are discouraged;
- Quickening the pace of developing industries using new and high technology, supporting the development of new industries and products.

A remarkable point in the "Outline" was its announcement of a state industrial organization policy. This policy aims to promote "rational competition", reap economies of scale and exploit coordinative specialization. For industries with strong scale economies, the document recommended a pro-large approach while for other industries it offered encouragement to small businesses.

This document also defined the authorities of industrial policy making, the examination and approval procedure for industrial policies. The state council is the authority that sets national industrial policies while the State Planning Commission is in charge of designing and coordinating sectoral industrial policies. The "Outline" required the establishment of a formal arrangement for implementing the policies and of a system to evaluate and monitor the outcomes of the policies.

Based on the "Outline", the State Planning Commission (SPC) has drafted sector-specific industrial policies for telecommunications, transportation, construction, electronics, machinery, petroleum processing and chemical material production. It has also masterminded the industrial policies regarding foreign investment, foreign trade, industrial organization and technology development.

An Open Door with Gate-keeping

Through the 1980s to the early 1990s, economic reform led to fundamental changes in the sources of investment in fixed capital (Table 4.3). While the share of state appropriation declined, the importance of foreign investment increased significantly. From 1985 to 1995, the proportion of foreign investment in domestic fixed capital investment increased from 3.6 per cent to 11.5 per cent. The total actualized foreign direct investment during the Eighth Five-Year Plan period (1991–95) reached US$ 114.7 billion, a 6.84-time increase over the amount of FDI invested during the Seventh Five-Year plan period.

Generally China has an official policy to encourage foreign investment in manufacturing with hi-tech features and investment in infrastructure development, such as transportation, telecommunication, and energy resources. Export-oriented projects and import-substitution projects are also preferred. Both the Seventh and Eighth Five-Year plans reflected these policies. The government carries out these policies mainly through exercising its approval authority over foreign-invested projects.

In the early 1980s, when China had just started to woo foreign investors, the government's attention was on removing obstacles that blocked inflows of foreign capital. Measures were designed to solve the problems such as the foreign-funded enterprises' difficulties in balancing their foreign exchange accounts due to the official policy of exchange controls. As the attraction of China's huge market potential increased to foreign investors, Beijing's attention focused more on how to utilize foreign capital more effectively to meet its national development priorities.

In the second half of the 1980s, the authorities introduced some performance requirements for foreign investors. One of these requirements was import substitution. Restrictions were put on imports of goods for which local equivalents were available and Chinese buyers were required to purchase from domestic suppliers. This policy was no longer officially practised after a Sino–US memorandum on market access was signed in 1992.

Another practice was the co-production agreements for foreign-invested projects, which require the vendor to produce a progressively greater proportion of the products in co-operation with a Chinese manufacturer. The foreign investor might also face pressures to increase the local content of its product in accordance with a timetable negotiated as part of the joint-venture contract.[22]

After China developed her first set of explicit industrial policies in 1989, the government increasingly used the country's vast market potential as leverage to lure foreign investment into areas prioritized by the state industrial policies. At the beginning of 1993, China planned a series of measures to attract foreign investment in the areas of finance, communications, information technology, farm products processing, urban infrastructure and housing renovation.[23]

FDI: Encouraged, Allowed, Restricted and Forbidden

The official guidelines toward foreign investors remained rather obscure until the State Planning Commission, Economic and Trade Commission and MOFTEC jointly promulgated the first explicit direction guide for foreign investment in June 1995.[24] In principle, the government divided foreign-funded projects into four categories: namely, the projects to be encouraged, the ones to be allowed, the ones to be restricted, and the ones to be forbidden.

The projects to be **encouraged** include:

- Projects that involve new agricultural techniques, comprehensive agriculture development, and development of energy, transportation and major raw materials;
- Projects that involve new and/or high-tech and thus can help save energy and raw materials, raise the technical level and economic efficiency;
- Projects that can meet the demand of the international market and help upgrade products and thus can help open up markets and expand exports;
- Projects that involve new technology and equipment for the comprehensive use of natural resources, and recycling of resources and prevention of environment pollution;
- Projects that can have a better use of manpower and natural resources in the central and western parts of the country, and accord with the state industrial policies;
- Other projects that are encouraged by state regulations or policies.

Projects to be encouraged can enjoy a range of preferential treatment as stipulated by state laws and administrative regulations. Besides, if the projects are connected with the construction and operation of energy and transportation infrastructure (coal, electricity, local railways, roads and ports) that require large investment and have long reimbursement periods, the investors can expand their business scope to related areas on state approval.

The projects to be **restricted** include:

- Projects with technologies that have been well developed domestically or already introduced from abroad; or projects that would add to a domestic production capacity that has already well satisfied domestic demand;

- Projects in sectors that are only open for foreign investment on a trial basis or are under state monopoly franchise;
- Projects that involve prospecting and exploiting rare and precious mineral resources;
- Projects that involve industries under the state unified planning;
- Other projects that are restricted by state laws and administrative regulations.

According to the State's industrial policies and needs arising from macroeconomic control, restricted foreign-funded projects are divided into sub-category A and sub-category B.

The restricted projects shall have a definite operation term. In the case of joint venture, the fixed assets put in by the Chinese side should come from the Chinese firm's own capital or assets (without involving using bank loans or raising funds).

Foreign investment is **prohibited** for projects that fall into any of the following categories:

- Projects that endanger the country's security or social and public interest;
- Projects that would cause environmental pollution or bring harm to natural resources and human health;
- Projects that have to occupy large tracts of farm land, are harmful to environment protection and development of land resources, and/or endanger the security of military facilities and their effective uses;
- Projects that have to use China's own special craftsmanship or indigenous skills for production;
- Other projects that are banned by the state law and administrative regulations.

Based on the above principles, the State Planning Commission regularly compiles, updates and promulgates the Guiding Catalogue of Industries for Foreign Investment. Government authorities' evaluation and approval of foreign-funded projects should be made in compliance with the Guiding Catalogue of Industries for Foreign Investment. Projects not belonging to the categories of being encouraged, restricted or forbidden are those in the category of the **allowed**. The first catalogue published in June 1995 covers 315 sectors.

Signs of Success

Data in Table 4.11 reflect the changes in sectoral distribution of the foreign direct investment in China during the period 1990–95. One can observe the unusual rise of foreign investment from 1992 to 1993. The amount of total foreign investment committed in 1993 rose by more than 90 per cent from the previous year. The investment in the real estate and public utility sector rose more than 140 per cent, contributing the lion's share of total growth.

Table 4.11 (I) *Amount and Share of (Contractual) Foreign Direct Investment by Sector (in US$ million)*

	1990	1991	1992	1993	1994	1995
Agriculture	122.25 1.85%	219.96 1.84%	678.13 1.17%	1,191.47 1.07%	972.45 1.18%	1,735.78 1.90%
Manufacturing	5,569.2 84.43%	9,622.69 80.34%	32,666.73 56.20%	51,173.68 45.92%	43,898.90 53.10%	61,647.63 67.54%
Construction	181.08 2.75%	134.20 1.12%	1,838.58 3.16%	3,878.37 3.48%	2,393.53 2.89%	1,918.36 2.10%
T.P.T	36.46 0.55%	94.95 0.79%	1,543.43 2.66%	1,489.91 1.34%	2,030.01 2.46%	1,696.98 1.86%
Commerce & catering	106.60 1.62%	174.24 1.45%	1,443.84 2.48%	4,606.47 4.13%	3,921.89 4.74%	3,426.65 3.75%
Real Estate & Public Utilities	452.47 6.86%	1,503.71 12.56%	18,079.64 31.11%	43,771.15 39.28%	23,861.51 28.86%	17,835.42 19.54%
Science & Technology	31.95 0.48%	18.55 0.15%	61.85 0.11%	587.75 0.53%	273.60 0.33%	277.75 0.30%
Other	128.07 1.94%	227.07 1.90%	1,873.16 3.22%	5,324.61 4.78%	5,601.48 6.77%	3,020.71 3.31%
Total	6,596.1	11,976.8	58,123.5	111,435.7	82,679.8	91,281.5

Note: "T.P.T" refers to "Transportation, Post, and Telecommunications".

Source: *Almanac of China's Foreign Economic and Commercial Relations*, various issues.

Underlining this phenomenal growth was an important political-economic event. In early 1992, Deng Xiaoping, the paramount leader of the CPC, called on the Party leadership during a tour to southern China to speed up economic reform and opening up to the world. The call was endorsed by the Party's Fourteenth National Congress held later in 1992 and led to a nationwide surge of fixed capital investment and economic growth.

The so-called "rolling development approach" was a major measure introduced in 1992 to speed up development of infrastructure and real estate. Local governments initiated real estate development plans by granting the user's right of sites to be developed to local real estate developers. These developers, usually government-linked, would then apply for bank loans to "clear the land" for further development. This usually involved compensating the residents for their relocating costs. Once this was done, the domestic developer would lease the land to foreign companies for more real estate developments. The domestic developers thus recovered the invested fund with hefty profits and would use the fund for the next round of "rolling development".[25]

Table 4.11 (II) *Number of (Contractual) Foreign Direct Investment Projects and Average Size by Sector*

	1990	1991	1992	1993	1994	1995
Agriculture	223	325	1,017	1,704	1,062	903
	0.548	*0.677*	*0.667*	*0.699*	*0.916*	*1.922*
Manufacturing	6,591	11,632	38,603	56,549	33,228	27,687
	0.845	*0.827*	*0.846*	*0.905*	*1.321*	*2.227*
Construction	43	77	1,125	3,167	1,531	944
	4.211	*1.743*	*1.634*	*1.225*	*1.563*	*2.032*
T.P.T	51	69	470	915	474	268
	0.715	*1.376*	*3.284*	*1.628*	*4.283*	*6.332*
Commerce &	96	236	1,505	4,842	3,117	1,851
catering	*1.110*	*0.738*	*0.959*	*0.951*	*1.258*	*1.851*
Real Estate &	158	401	4,536	11,322	5,180	3,279
Public Utilities	*2.864*	*3.750*	*3.986*	*3.866*	*4.606*	*5.439*
Science &	24	66	223	881	469	275
Technology	*1.331*	*0.281*	*0.277*	*0.667*	*0.583*	*1.010*
Other	111	238	1,508	4,938	2,957	2,079
	1.154	*0.954*	*1.242*	*1.078*	*1.894*	*1.453*
Total	7,273	12,978	48,764	83,437	47,549	37,011
	0.907	*0.923*	*1.192*	*1.336*	*1.739*	*2.466*

Notes:

a. Figures in italics are average project sizes in US$ million.

b. "T.P.T" refers to "Transportation, Post, and Telecommunications".

Source: *Almanac of China's Foreign Economic and Commercial Relations*, various issues.

Many local governments regarded the "rolling development approach" as a big success since it required only a relatively small amount of initial capital to start a series of development projects. The practice, however, amidst rampant business speculation and bureaucratic corruption, soon led to a real estate glut.

Alarmed by signs of macroeconomic overheating, the central government imposed tighter controls on bank loans in 1993–94 to cool the economy. In early 1995, Beijing announced three measures to hold up the nationwide "rolling development". These included suspending approval of high-class commercial real estate projects for one year, suspending loans to any newly started projects, and cancelling exemption from import duties for 20 types of office equipment used for these projects.

These retrenchment measures, together with industrial policies to encourage investment in prioritized sectors, led to significant changes in the foreign direct investment structure. The proportion of FDI in construction, real estate and public utilities slumped in 1994 and 1995. Apart from the episode of "rolling development", we can identify some achievements of China's industrial policies toward foreign direct investment (see Table 4. 11(II)).

First, the amount and share of foreign investment in transportation, postal and telecommunications increased after 1992 and remained high throughout 1995. Second, the amount pledged in science and technology rose remarkably for the years 1993 to 1995. Investment in agriculture also recovered in 1995 in terms of amount and shares. Third, except for "construction" and "science and technology", almost all sectors displayed a trend toward larger average project sizes. For sectors such as "transportation and telecommunications" and "real estate and utilities", the larger average project size may indicate a higher proportion of investment in infrastructure development. The rise of average size in the manufacturing sector may indicate that projects with high-tech features or with greater capital intensity were developed.

The rising average size of foreign-invested projects has been an on-going trend since the 1980s. In the period 1986-90, the average size of contractual FDI projects was US$ 1.06 million. The figure rose to US$ 1.53 million for the period 1991-95. China's industrial policy to attract large transnational corporations in capital- or technology-intensive projects has played a pivotal role in these changes.

NOTES

1. *China Economic Yearbook* 1981, p. III-37.
2. For an original discussion on socialist material balance planning, see Montias (1959).
3. People's Daily et al. (1991), p. 74; *China Statistical Yearbook* 1992, p. 158.
4. Lin et al. (1996), pp. 39–44.
5. See Lu (1994a), pp. 78–91 for a summary of Mao's economic thoughts.
6. Donnithorne (1972).
7. World Bank (1984).
8. Jia and Tisdell (1996).
9. Zhao ed. (1989), p. 193, p. 349.
10. Zhao ed. (1989), pp. 388–391.
11. *Documents of the Fourth Session of the Fifth National People's Congress*, Beijing: People's Press, 1981.
12. Long March was the journey of 9,660 km. undertaken by the Red Army of China in 1934–35. After a major defeat by the Nationalist forces in Jiangxi, a province in southeast China, some 90,000 men and women of the Red Army marched west to Guizhou province. Led by Mao, they then pushed on to Shaanxi province in northwest China despite natural obstacles and harassment by Nationalist troops. More than half the marchers were lost in this almost incredible one-year trek.
13. *Documents of the Twelfth National Congress of the CPC*, Beijing: People's Press, 1982.
14. See Table 4.3 for a definition of primary, secondary and tertiary industries.
15. Zhao ed. (1989), p. 515 and Zhu (1993).
16. Li Peng, "Report on the Ten-Year Guideline Plan of National Economic and Social Development and the Eighth Five-Year Plan", *People's Daily* (Beijing), 11 April 1991.
17. *Zhongguo Jingji Nianjian* [Almanac of China's Economy] 1990, pp. I: 55–59.
18. "The Outline of the Ten-Year Guideline Plan of National Economic and Social Development and the Eighth Five-Year Plan", in *Almanac of China's Economy*, 1991, pp. I: 47–73.
19. Based on the same principle, the state has also promulgated a list of forbidden projects.
20. State Council, "The Provisional Regulation on the PRC's Direction-Adjustment Tax on Fixed Capital Investment" (16 April 1991), Zhang and Wu (1994), pp. 584–605.
21. *Renmin Ribao* [People's Daily], Beijing, 23 June 1994.
22. *East Asian Executive Reports*, May 1994, pp. 12–13.
23. Trade and Development Board, *Trade and Investment Guide: China*, Singapore: Arther Anderson, 1993, p. 120.
24. *China Economic News*, Beijing, 24 July 1995.
25. Wang X, "Structural Change of FDI in China", *Lianhe Zaobao* [United Morning Post], Singapore, 31 July 1995.

5. Uncertainty in Preferential Policies

5.1 THE UNCERTAIN BUSINESS

There surely have been a lot of changes in China's preferential policies over the years, as discussed in the previous chapters. For businessmen and investors, the most disturbing nature of the system is not the changes but the uncertainty in terms of policy interpretation and enforcement. In the contemporary Chinese business environment, as noted by an American businessman, "it does no matter much how the law says but how the person sitting in the government office who interprets the law would say".[1]

The administrative uncertainty related to preferential policies is a serious problem. In the eyes of foreign investors, China has become "a sort of Shangri-La where the basic laws of commerce – contracts, property rights, the rule of law – are suspended and profits are had by tossing in ever higher sums of money".[2] Even Li Ka-shing, the Hong Kong business tycoon who has gainfully ridden on China's recent economic boom, has complained about unfair competition in China's business environment. He observed that "central and regional taxations show a lack of clarity". "State policies are frequently amended". "The process of reviewing and approving projects is rather complicated" and "the different legal, accounting, and financing systems also add to the difficulty of investing in China".[3]

Soft Constraints

Such administrative uncertainty is due to fact that legitimate authority of government bureaucrats are not effectively constrained by law. This phenomenon presents the political–economy context of the soft budget constraint problem in the state sector.

Kornai (1980) first proposed the concept of "soft budget constraint" of socialist state-owned enterprises (SOEs) in his study of commodity shortage in centrally planned economies. As observed by Kornai, the centrally planned socialist economy is a system of shortage, where commodity shortage is a systemic, perpetual, and self-reproducing condition. The shortage arises from the nature of the socialist enterprises, which operate under fundamentally different rules from capitalist enterprises.

In a capitalist market economy, the firm maximizes profit under its budget constraint, under which the firm lives within its means and bears the full risks of running its business. A capitalist enterprise that fails to live within its means would be insolvent and punished by bankruptcy. In that sense, a capitalist enterprise has a "hard budget constraint", which defines the firm's spending limit and keeps the firm accountable for its conduct. The hard budget constraint constantly polices all capitalist firms' activities and forces them to follow the first law of doing business: to be competitive and efficient or go bust.

In contrast, in a pre-reform centrally planned command economy, the entry, exit, expansion and contraction of the enterprise do not depend on its profitability. It is the central planners, not the market, who decide if a firm or even a whole sector should survive and expand. Given distorted prices and centrally planned resource allocation, profitability is never a good indicator of the firm's performance efficiency. Therefore, the financial fitness of a state-owned enterprise is always secondary to the firm's capability to fulfil the planned targets. Budget constraints do not need to be binding upon the firm. The ultimate norm that a firm must follow is the fulfilment of centrally planned targets for its physical outputs, rather than maintaining profitability and financial fitness.

In a post-reform socialist economy, the "soft budget constraint" phenomenon becomes even more manifest. Since the SOEs are the creations of the state, the state bureaucracy exhibits a paternalistic attitude towards the SOEs. Kornai (1986) pointed out that the post-reform Hungarian economy in the mid-1980s was suffering from the "soft budget constraint syndrome". Although economic reforms brought in some financial discipline to the SOEs, the budget constraint was still not effective and could be "stretched" at the will of the administrative authorities.

Roots of Administrative Uncertainty

In a discussion of the post-socialist transition in Hungary, Kornai (1992) urged for a strong and persistent effort to repress the former hyper-activity of the state. Obviously, governmental officials' interventionist conduct and its uncertainty continue to be the basis for soft budget constraint and an obstacle to business efficiency.

It is noteworthy that the state sector's soft budget constraint has its counterpart in the political sphere: *the soft authority constraint.* This concept refers to the poorly defined allocation of legitimate authority among the major components of the political hierarchy in transition economies. The softness of the authority constraint allows irregular use of public money and power for intervention into firms' business activity. This provides opportunities for rent seeking by officials who have vested interests in maintaining the soft budget constraint of state-owned enterprises. Therefore the poorly defined allocation of administrative authority has significant implications on the economic transition towards a market economy.

The soft authority constraint is a legacy of the pre-reform socialist system. In such a system, the ruling Communist Party's political accountability is not held by a stable system of public choice. The Party dominates all important functions of the state, including those of administration, legislation and jurisdiction. The highly centralized decision making and the hierarchical control structure in the Party are the backbone of the centrally planned socialist economic system. The government–business relationship is of the type whereby the central planner commands and controls the enterprise.

During transition to a market economy, economic reforms have decentralized and delegated decision making to local levels. On the one hand, the emergence of the market economy has significantly weakened the Party's control over the social economic life (as in China and Vietnam) or even led to the birth of a parliamentary democracy (as in Russia and other former Soviet states). On the other hand, the political infrastructure compatible with a modern market economy has yet to be developed. The government–business relationship needs to be redefined by a new legal framework based on the sanctity of property rights. Such a legal framework needs time to develop and requires a functional and independent judicial system to be enforced.

Meanwhile it takes time to change the mind-set of central planning for thousands of bureaucrats at all government levels. Before the completion of this difficult transition, confusions and uncertainty over government officials' authority toward business are inevitable. Consequently, bureaucrats gain greater discretion in interpreting their own legitimate authorities. Similar to the phenomenon of soft budget constraints for firms, the legal constraints on government officials' administrative authority do not bind effectively. To some extent, they can be "stretched" at will by the officials who liberally interpret their own legitimate authorities.

5.2 POLITICAL ECONOMY OF POLICY UNCERTAINTY

The Party and the State

There are several sources of soft authority constraint in China. The most important one is the Leninist Party–state structure. The Communist Party of

China (CPC) is the only ruling party defined and assured by the Constitution of the People's Republic of China (PRC). The Party has absolute control over the administration and the army. Party organizations parallel the structure of government. At all levels Party and government authorities overlap and interlock with one another, with Party members monitoring government activities.[4]

All legislative changes and major jurisdictory decisions originate from the Party. Within the Party, decisions are made in a hierarchic power structure with the top leadership having the ultimate power to delegate or withdraw authorities of lower echelons. Meanwhile, Party policies have quasi-legal status. They can take effect before the introduction of legislative formalities and lay down the foundation for new laws. Law is seen as a mature form of Party policy.[5] Legislative changes have usually been made to meet the changes of the Party's guidelines. The State Council's "Decision on Clearing the Regulations and By-laws" in 1983, for instance, asserted that the legislative changes should be made according to the current guidelines and policies of the Party.[6]

In the Leninist Party–state structure, the Communist Party is not only the sole source of the law but also the ultimate interpreter of the law. In the PRC, the term "*sifa jiguan*" [judicial organs] refers to government agents concerned with the application of the law. Judicial organs include the people's courts, the people's procuratorates, the public security and state security organs, and the organs of judicial administration.[7] The functions performed by the judicial organs are called the "*zheng fa gongzuo*" [political-legal work]. The political-legal work is under the control and leadership of the CPC. Under the CPC Central Committee, there exists a central political-legal committee, usually headed by a member of the Politburo Standing Committee. Within each Party committee at each administration level, such as the provincial Party committee or county Party committee, there is a member who specializes in political-legal matters or works with a political-legal subcommittee or group under the Party committee. The subcommittee or group would consist of the heads of the all judicial organs, including the courts at the relevant provincial or local level.[8] In other words, at each administrative level, the court is under the leadership of the political-legal committee, which is in turn under the control of the Party committee at that level. Within this system it is difficult to ensure the full autonomy and independence of the judiciary. The legal constraints on administrative authority are inherently weak and soft.

An Ancient Tradition

The soft authority constraint of the Leninist Party–state structure is highly compatible with the Chinese bureaucratic tradition. The Chinese bureaucracy was one of the world's oldest with a millenarian history of laws and regulations. However, the ancient Chinese legal system had two distinctive features. First, there was at least one party, the emperor, standing above the law. The emperor and the officials he appointed had an absolute right to rule and the people were under an absolute obligation to obey. The emperor enjoyed the supreme legislative, judicial and executive powers. He made laws, which were binding on all subjects except the emperor himself. The emperor could alter the laws by decree at any time. He could also alter judgments or orders given by other judicial authorities.[9]

The second feature was power integration. Under Confucian tradition, rulers were expected to "rule by virtues", governing paternally in the people's interests. On top of the bureaucratic hierarchy, the imperial court under the emperor integrated the functions of highest administration, legislature and judicial authority. Even at levels below the imperial court, there was no developed doctrine of judicial independence. The governor of a province, prefecture or county was supposed to act as "*fumu guan*" [parent–officials] over their "*zimin*" [children–citizens]. He was simultaneously the head of local administration, the chief district judge and even the local legislator. Under this highly integrated power structure, the bureaucracy was hardly subject to checks and balances.[10] There was virtually no public awareness of governmental power being limited by law, or of individual rights enforceable against the state or other authorities in the social hierarchy. This tradition has had profound impact on the phenomenon of soft authority constraints in today's Chinese society.

Experiments with Trials and Errors

The experimental nature of China's gradualist reform in the 1980s also contributed to the softness of authority constraints. China's economic reform started in 1978–79 when the country was struggling to recover from the economic disarray caused by the chaotic Cultural Revolution (1966–76). Throughout the 1980s, facing ideological constraints and resistance from the old system, China's reformers had to take a "trial-and-error" approach.

Deng Xiaoping, the paramount leader of the Party, vividly described the approach as "crossing the river while groping for stones planted at the bottom".[11] An important strategy that has minimized and diversified the political and economic risks of reform was called the policy of "*shidian*", which literally means "experimental grounds". Under this policy, reforms should be first experimented within selected enterprises, sectors or regions. If a scheme works at the local level, the top leadership would promote it to the whole nation. If it does not, the leadership would bury it without inviting too much political fuss. Meanwhile the top leadership delegated greater autonomy to provincial and local governments to experiment with their own reforms. A consequence of experimental reform is the liberal interpretation of the legal limits of administrative power.

The legal framework inherited from the pre-reform era was mainly built according to the principles of traditional central planning. When the market-oriented reform started, many obsolete laws acted as a strait-jacket for reformers. A widespread saying in the mid-1980s expressed the frustration: "What looks reasonable may be illegal, what is legal looks really unreasonable". During the rapid reforms, legislative actions have often lagged behind the implementation of new policies. Most of the do's and don'ts were not defined by the laws but by the Party's or State Council's documents in the form of "Central Committee Circulars", "Temporary Regulations" and "Temporary Provisions". Policies are sometimes implemented without any legal basis, and existing laws are sometimes put aside, ignored or bent when new policies supersede those upon which the laws were based. In addition, reforms in many areas were initiated from below. Some initially "illegal" activities won official approval only after they became a prevailing *fait accompli* and turned out to be harmless. The government made ex post institutional changes to accommodate reforms from below.[12]

Bargaining for Better Deals

One feature of the Leninist Party–state structure is the constant bargaining for authorities within the political hierarchy. Bargaining politics greatly softens authority constraints on administrative powers. Many rights and responsibilities of governmental organs and bureaucrats are not defined by law but subject to political bargaining and negotiations.

The economic roots of the bargaining politics lie in the central planning nature of a command economy. In such an economy, decision making on resource allocation is highly centralized. It is the central planners, rather than the market demand and supply, that determine what to produce, how to produce, and how to distribute income and wealth. Coordination of productive activities among thousands of factories and farms relies predominantly on vertical channels of communication and control. Without a market economy, central planning has to achieve internal consistency between planned supplies and planned demands for goods and services within the planning hierarchy. For this purpose, central planners construct a large number of "material balances" for a wide variety of raw and semi-finished materials, fuels and equipment. Such a material balancing process has to be built on the lower echelons' claims for input needs to fulfil the planned targets. Since bureaucrat managers' performance is evaluated according to their capability to fulfil planned targets, they tend to bargain for an "easier" plan with more modest output assignments and more generous input authorizations. By over-claiming for input requirements and by hoarding production capacity, the lower-level managers can make their own job easier and life less stressful. Contrarily, high-level planners' task is to maintain an economy-wide material balance while aiming at ambitious output targets. To minimize the slack in their domain, the higher-level officials endeavour to impose a "taut" combination of output assignments and input authorizations on the lower echelons. Therefore bargaining is inevitable between the enterprise and the supervisory department, between the department and the ministry, and between the ministry and the central agencies over planning details.[13]

This bargaining tradition continues to influence economic decision making in the post-reform era. Decentralization of decision making was the major measure taken by Beijing in the early stage of reform to invigorate the economy. Managers of SOEs were delegated more decision-making rights over their daily business and encouraged to seek profit in markets. Local governments were granted greater autonomy to take care of their own budgets.

In 1980 China introduced the "Budget Revenue Sharing System", which set the local governments' specific shares of financial revenues and responsibility for meeting the revenue targets of central government. To a large extent, the revenue-sharing system hardened the local governments' budget constraints and provided great incentives for the latter to increase their revenues. Under the system, however, the fiscal rights and responsibilities of governments of different levels were not defined by law. Bargaining between the central and local governments was the major process to compromise different interests over revenue-sharing ratios, budget subsidies and expenditure quotas.[14] In the process, the local governments with better connections with Beijing usually won better deals. Regions of greater economic or political importance also tended to gain by taking advantage of their higher bargaining power. These factors contributed to the deteriorating inter-region inequality in the reform era.

The bargaining tradition also circumvented reforms to harden the budget constraints of SOEs. A major reform in the mid-1980s replaced the profit-remittance system with a corporate-income taxation system for SOEs. The move was a bid to make SOEs financially independent. It was expected that with this tax-for-profit reform, the relationship between SOEs and the state would be reduced to that between the taxpayer and the tax collector. In practice, however, the local authorities could set the effective tax rates by deciding each enterprise's tax base. Driven by their own interests, enterprise managers would bargain for better tax arrangements. In the mid-1980s when the price distortions were common, it was convenient for enterprise managers to blame their low profits or losses on external factors and demand for compensatory tax arrangements. Local officials tended to accommodate the demand because corporate income tax revenue was shared between the local and central governments. The revenue loss due to generous tax arrangements could be made up by collecting other local business levies. Therefore effective tax rates were tailored to the profitability of each enterprise. The reform ended up with a "soft taxation" scheme subject to an arbitrary process of bargaining between the bureaucrats and managers.[15] Again in this process, enterprises with better connections in local government or with higher bargaining power were likely to get better deals.

5.3 WHO ARE THE REAL PREFERRED?

In the early days of reforms, the uncertain authority of the bureaucratic system might have provided flexibility to policy making and expedited some reforms. As the transition toward a market economy continues, however, the negative impact of this institutional feature has become more perceptible.

The Local Nest

Since public authorities that command fiscal resources do not face hard constraints, the budget constraints of governmental organs and their associated SOEs could not be hardened. For instance, the fiscal decentralization in the early 1980s authorized local governments in charge of tax collection and administration. Rather than sharing the tax revenue with the centre, local governments have pursued tax evasion or avoidance tactics to keep revenues within the area. In Jiangsu province, town governments allow (or actually "condone") the accounting malpractice of keeping two books in local firms. One is for "*zhangmian lirun*" [book profit], which is the base for tax-collecting agencies to calculate tax payable; the other is for "*jiesuan lirun*" [accounting profit], which is used to calculate the payments to the town government and employees' bonuses. The "accounting profit" is always larger than the "book profit" if there is no tax exemption.[16]

The local government and enterprises may also collaborate against the centre's efforts to control investment and consumption funds. By manipulating the effective tax rates and financial treatment toward local enterprises, the local government can help the enterprises retain a larger portion of their earnings. Funds "stored" in this way in the enterprises can then be transferred to local fiscal revenue by ad hoc levies. There is no hard constraint on the local government's legitimate authority to impose such levies. The retained money also goes to the local government's coffer through local firms' "voluntary" contributions or "apportionment" for local projects. Besides the "soft taxation" scheme and administrative levies on the retained earnings, the local government also possesses the power to press local banks to provide "interest free loans" or "subsidized interest loans" (negative-interest loans) to local businesses. All these activities have led to an explosive growth of extra-budgetary revenues in local government coffers.[17]

The Chronic Loss-Making Problem

The soft constraint of local authority and budget has been a main barrier to SOE reform. As mentioned in the previous section, negotiation and bargaining for special tax arrangements have circumvented reforms to harden budget constraints of SOEs. Meanwhile, by linking local revenues directly to enterprise income, fiscal decentralization pushed SOEs under the closer care of local governments. Therefore, for managers of SOEs, bargaining for favourable financial treatment from local authorities became an attractive alternative to seeking profits by improving management. They would devote much of their effort to winning bureaucratic favours, an unproductive use of their resources. The risk of being inefficient is, however, not fully borne by the SOE managers due to the poor accountability of their business.

Loss-making SOEs have been a chronic problem of the Chinese economy in the past decade. According to surveys by the government, about 40 per cent of SOEs were in the red in 1996. The SOEs' debts accounted for 85 per cent of their assets on average.[18] China's Law of Bankruptcy, which was supposed to have been in effect since 1988, has yet to act as a hard constraint for many loss-making SOEs. Fearful of the widespread unemployment of millions, the government has postponed indefinitely nationwide bankruptcy reforms. To solve the SOE debt problem, the government introduced asset ownership reforms in 1993 in a bid to liquidate the assets of ailing SOEs. Unfortunately, under weak accountability and soft authority constraints, the reform was abused by many. Even profitable SOEs got in on the act. A cosmetic restructuring exercise divided the spoils among managers and employees. Insiders profited from the sale of shares. Some firms sold their assets at prices way below market values to woo foreign investors. These activities have resulted in the serious erosion of state assets, which was estimated at about Rmb 100 billion a year at the mid-1990s.[19] The bankruptcy reform itself has already been abused. In a prefecture of Shanxi Province, the local government colluded with the local court to announce the bankruptcy of a local SOE. By doing so, the local government "cleared" itself dozens of million-Rmb debts liable to state banks and enterprises in other regions.[20]

Bureaucratic Rent Seeking

Rent seeking in the political area is another major consequence of the weak constraint on administrative authority. There are ample opportunities for bureaucrats to seek contrived economic rents since rules and regulations have not been transparent and clear enough to determine how the government should interface with business.

Until the end of 1993, China did not have a unified company law governing the formation, organization and termination of companies. The power of approving the establishment of companies was vested in various functional administrative agencies inherited from the central planning hierarchy. Applications with official backing would usually have an advantage in the process. During fiscal decentralization, governments of various levels were called upon to be responsible for their own revenues. They would naturally try to profit from their approving and licensing powers for new companies. The result was the emergence and growth of "administrative companies", which were established by various levels of governmental departments or Party organizations.[21] With privileges and powers, those government-linked companies were in a strong position to reap profits by collecting economic rents from the market-oriented transition. In 1992, they accounted for 10 per cent of the 1.25 million newly registered enterprises. Direct involvement in business has had profound implications on the economic role of government.[22]

The abuse of administrative power ranges from the widespread practice of "local protectionism" to the local backing of illegal stock markets. Given the incentives to keep fiscal revenues within one's own regime, virtually all levels of local governments have in varying degrees imposed barriers that prevent or impede access to their local markets.[23] Some local authorities even erected check points along regional blockades to prevent some local resources from moving to other provinces and to bar some products of other regions from competing with local ones. Various forms of illegal stock markets have been reported to be operating vigorously in some Chinese cities.[24] Huge amounts of state funds were reportedly used in speculative trades on stock markets.[25] Many of these illegal activities were backed by local authorities. Jiang Zemin, the head of the CPC, admitted that "Protectionism in some local governments and departments has become a serious problem as many pretend to comply but oppose covertly".[26]

Local government-backed tax evasion has still been rampant even after China introduced a major tax reform in 1994. The comprehensive 1994 tax reform attempted to reduce the local incentives to protect local markets and develop administrative companies. It aimed to build within five years a three-tiered federalized system of taxation similar to that in the US. The overall goal of the reform is to codify the fiscal rights and responsibilities of governments, enterprises and individuals by creating a fair and equitable system of taxation based on standard international practices.[27] Thanks to the reform, tax revenue shot up by more than 25 per cent in 1994. A nationwide survey by the Ministry of Finance nevertheless found that the amount of evaded taxes increased by 26.2 per cent in the same year. According to the State Administration of Taxation, many local governments continue to retain money in their regimes by altering tax rates or tax bases without authorization. Some ignore the new tax system and collect taxes under the old rules. Improper handling of invoices in value-added tax collection is not unusual. Some localities give tax exemptions, allow tax delays and grant tax refunds without going through proper procedures to obtain central government's authorization.[28]

Bureaucratic corruption is the most manifest rent-seeking activity in contemporary China. The soft authority constraint provides the possibility for bureaucrats to create and manipulate contrived scarcity and its associated rent with low risks of being punished. As reform revived the private economy and greatly increased general freedom in daily economic life, possession of transferable property rights and accumulation of personal wealth became feasible. These have led to the rapid growth of bureaucratic corruption. In the 15 years after China started economic reform, the Chinese economy achieved a 9 per cent average annual growth rate and nearly quadrupled its GNP. However, economic crimes have grown at an even faster pace. In the 1980s, the number of cases of economic crimes accepted by procuratorial organs increased nine times with an average annual growth rate of 24.57 per cent.[29] Corruption cases accounted for a major percentage of the economic cases. The growth of corruption has continued to outpace economic growth in the 1990s. Take 1994 for example: nationwide corruption cases increased by nearly 70 per cent, a growth rate much higher than the 11.8 per cent growth rate of GDP.[30] China's top prosecutor, Zhang Siqing, pointed out that current corruption was the worst since the PRC was founded in 1949. "Embezzlement and bribery, covering huge sums of illicit money, are now typical of crimes which chiefly involve people in 'powerful' positions".[31] Between 1987 and 1992, at least Rmb 3,000 billion of SOE assets went missing due to bureaucratic corruption.[32] During 1982 to 1994, a total of Rmb 18.1 billion went missing from Beijing municipal coffers. The amount is equivalent to 16.75 per cent of Beijing's 1994 GDP.[33]

Widespread rent seeking and bureaucratic corruption imply an inefficient civil service, which leads to high transaction costs of doing business. To have business done through a corrupt civil service is costly. A Singapore businessman estimates that for each of his projects in China, he has to allot 15 per cent of total costs for entertaining officials, staff pilferage and general inefficiencies.[34]

Lax Laws

In the first place, China's legislation has been lagging behind the needs of reform and development in many areas. As explained in the previous section, in the process of bottom-up reform, innovative reformers and private entrepreneurs repeatedly violated official restrictions in the form of obsolete laws and regulations. These activities were followed by ex post institutional innovations and changes which accommodated the new practices. During this process, people might have lost respect for existing laws. Even the government looks to legislation as a tool to implement the Party's policies.

Compared with the inadequacies of the legislation, ineffectiveness of enforcement is a more serious problem. A US trade official observed that, although China has markedly improved its intellectual-property-rights legislation in recent years, "the enforcement of intellectual property rights has been virtually absent, with piracy rates soaring in all major urban centres along China's increasingly prosperous east coast".[35] A Chinese official also admitted that "China's legal measures outpace the ability of the authorities to enforce them".[36] Striking gaps exist between the law as stated in the statute book and actual behaviour on the part of officials and citizens. A survey in the late 1980s showed that only 10 per cent of all existing laws were being effectively enforced, 20 per cent were implemented fairly, 50 per cent were enforced with difficulty, and 20 per cent were ineffective.[37] Severe shortage of professional personnel in legal business is a major reason for the slack enforcement of laws.

The rapid transition of the legal framework and slack enforcement of new laws have resulted in a social cynicism toward law and order.[38] Foreign businesspersons in China are often bewildered by their Chinese counterparts' and officials' "flexible approach to the law" and "literal interpretation" of legal terms. The "negotiable regulation" and numerous unpublished laws and regulations also make business prospects uncertain.[39] The social psychology of "everything is negotiable anytime" is widespread among officials.

Rampant tax evasion also reflects the social cynicism toward law and order. According to state media, from 1985 to 1996, the government authorities uncovered tax, auditing and pricing violations valued at Rmb 161 billion, an average of Rmb 14.6 billion a year. This was about 4 per cent of the average annual government revenue. Up to 60 per cent of state-owned or collective firms evaded taxes. By 1996, taxpayers had evaded personal income tax worth an estimated Rmb 12 billion since the tax was introduced in 1990.[40]

As for foreign investment, local government officials consistently try to keep project approval away from the Ministry of Foreign Trade and Economic Cooperation (MOFTEC) and other central ministries. Under a threshold rule set by MOFTEC, large projects must get central government approval. To bypass the rule, the local authorities often play diversionary tactics. They may divide the investment of a large project into several investment phases to reduce the amount that needs approval. After they get approval, they may increase the investment amount and merge the approved smaller projects into one. Local authorities may also establish separate legal investor entities to cover the real sources of capital to make it easier to get project approval.[41]

Booms and Busts

Soft constraints on administrative authority aggravated macroeconomic instability, a serious systemic problem of the Chinese economy. As noted by Wong and Chen (1995), local governments, with their extra-budgetary fiscal resources, often openly or indirectly undermine or counteract the central government's efforts to implement tight monetary and fiscal policies.

Until recently, when there was a clash of policy objectives between the centre and local governments, the latter would almost always have the upper hand. The local governments, under soft constraints on their authorities, may continue to use their extra-budgetary fiscal resources to pursue ambitious expansion programmes despite nation–wide macroeconomic conditions.

Bargaining politics not only determines the fiscal resource allocation between the centre and the local governments but also influences the money supply in the economy. This is because China's banking system still follows centrally planned credit allocation. The credit plan is accommodating to the overall planning process and developed "from bottom up". Local authorities submit their credit needs, which then become the subject of negotiations with the central government. Being squeezed between the demands of the central government and local authorities, the banking system is unable to serve as an independent, decentralized funding source.

Heading Toward "Rule of Law"

Despite the systemic defects we have discussed, today's political structure in China has already been significantly improved in the past 18 years of economic reform. One should not overlook the fact that there are far-reaching institutional rearrangements under way to move China into a more efficient and more formalized system of checks and balances. As observed by Heilmann (1995), politico-institutional changes have happened in the following four key areas:

- In the CPC's personnel system, new standards and procedures are emerging. Initial steps are taken to build a more institutionalized, less personalized and less manipulatable system of meritocracy;
- Meanwhile the assertiveness of the People's Congresses at all levels has been growing. The CPC leadership is promoting legislative bodies' quasi-parliamentary supervision of governments;
- In central–local relations, the Party–state command hierarchy has given way to a complex web of bargaining relations. This multi-layered bargaining system of decision making is a historical progression from the Maoist totalitarian command hierarchy;
- In social organizations, thousands of national and local economic and societal associations have emerged. There has already begun a gradual devolution of the one-Party control mechanisms to those specialized organizations.

These changes indicate that serious political efforts are being undertaken to reduce the scope of arbitrary "rule by person" and move the system to the rule of law. There are reasons to be optimistic about the prospects for this trend. The Leninist Party–state structure has been gradually worn away. As China opens to the world in an information age, the traditional social attitude towards law and order has to change. The CPC adoption of a wholesale programme to transform the country into a "socialist market economy" in 1992 marked the end of ideological constraints on economic reform. Transition toward market economy is no longer on a trial-and-error track. Top-down systematic institutional reforms have come to dominate local piecemeal experiments in the past three years.

The most manifest events in the economic area have been the 1994 Tax Reform and the two bank laws promulgated in 1995. The 1994 Tax Reform redefined central–local fiscal responsibility in a multi-tiered federalized system while the two bank laws aim to ensure the independence of the Central Bank and the independent commercial status of other major banks. Economic legislation in major fields has been accelerated to establish a legal framework for the country's socialist market economy. In a bid to tackle graft and bureaucratic corruption, the Ministry of Labour and Personnel introduced several important reforms in 1996. These reforms include banning government officials from giving jobs to relatives, avoiding family members working in certain departments if a relative is a supervisor, rotating top officials every five years, and setting up a top watch-dog institution against graft.

The central government also took measures to impose stricter constraints on local government's authority to collect levies. For instance, in December 1996, the State Planning Commission and Ministry of Finance jointly issued a circular to cancel 48 local government levies on construction projects. The document also established the regulation that local governments should publish the list of levies at regular intervals. All major levies should get approval from the State Council.[42]

The main barrier toward rule of law is physical rather than ideological. The speedy legislative work to build a modern legal framework has added pressures on an already creaky and feeble legal infrastructure. Chinese society has a short history of legal system building and hence lacks the experience and tradition of abiding by and enforcing laws. The most serious bottleneck is the severe shortage of trained legal personnel, which leaves many promulgated laws poorly enforced. This bottleneck is impossible to remove in the immediate future. Serious efforts, however, should be undertaken to professionalize judges and make the Chinese judiciary fully independent from administration.

NOTES

1. The businessman was the marketing manager of the American retailer, Pricemart. *Yazhou Zhoukan* [The International Chinese Newsweekly], Hong Kong, 10–16 March 1997, p. 15.
2. *Far Eastern Economic Review*, Hong Kong, 8 December 1994, p. 5.
3. Ibid.
4. Shirk (1992).
5. See Beijing University, Department of Law (1989), p. 49 and Keller (1989).
6. *Almanac of China's Economy* 1984, IV, p. 70; *Yearbook on Chinese Communism* 1989, VI, p. 81.
7. Du and Zhang (1990), p. 79.
8. Chen (1992), p. 106.
9. Chen (1992), p. 13.
10. Chen (1992), p. 13; Nathan (1985), p. 114.
11. Xinhua News Agency, 14 September 1986.
12. See Chen (1992), p. 94; Naughton (1994); and Lu (1994a), pp. 126, 158.
13. Bornstein (1989).
14. Wong and Chen (1995).
15. Walder (1992).

16. Wong, et al. (1995), p. 49.
17. See Wong (1991) and Blejer and Szapary (1990).
18. Reuter, *Straits Times*, Singapore, 7 October 1996, p. 47; AFP, *Straits Times*, Singapore, 28 January 1997, p. 37.
19. Gao (1995).
20. *Yazhou Zhoukan* [International Chinese Newsweekly], Hong Kong, 19 March 1995.
21. Lu (1994b), pp. 159–160.
22. Wong and Chen (1995), p. 126.
23. Chen K. (1991).
24. *Straits Times*, Singapore, 1 November 1993, p. 27.
25. *Yazhou Zhoukan* (International Chinese Newsweekly), Hong Kong, 4 June 1995.
26. *Qiu Shi* [Seeking the Truth], Beijing, 1 July 1996.
27. Brudvig (1994).
28. Yu (1995); Xinhua News Agency, *Straits Times*, Singapore, 24 March 1995.
29. Lu (1994a), p. 182.
30. *Lianhe Zaobao* [United Morning Post], Singapore, 3 August 1995.
31. Reuter, *Straits Times*, Singapore, 30 October 1993, p. 7.
32. *Lianhe Zaobao* [United Morning Post], Singapore, 23 September 1995, p. 26.
33. AFP, *Straits Times*, Singapore, 5 October 1995.
34. *Sunday Times*, Singapore, 8 October 1995.
35. USIS Info Packet, USTR China IPR fact sheet (2110), 5 February 1995.
36. *Economist*, UK, 7 January 1995, p. 53.
37. Chen (1992), pp. 92–93.
38. Lu D. (1994a), p. 158.
39. Fischer (1993).
40. Reuter, *Straits Times*, Singapore, 25 December 1996.
41. Howson (1995).
42. Xinhua News Agency, *Lianhe Zaobao* [United Morning Post], Singapore, 3 January 1997, p. 30.

6. Epilogue: Prospects of Preferential Policies

6.1 NEW DIRECTION OF STATE INTERVENTION

Since China started economic reform by the end of the 1970s, the Chinese economy has sustained a spectacular annual growth rate close to 10 per cent for nearly two decades. Meanwhile the mainly gradualist approach of reform has accumulated enough institutional changes to have transformed the economic system irreversibly toward a market economy. One of the critical institutional changes has been the new orientation of the state's role in the economy.

More Friendly to Market

On the whole, economic reform has greatly reduced the previously all-encompassing role of the government as a central planner of a command economy. After abolishing mandatory planning in the 1980s, the Chinese government has reoriented its economic role to be more "market-friendly".[1]

It has put great efforts into building social institutions (including the legal framework) compatible to a market economy. Its attention has been more focused on maintaining macroeconomic stability and construction of infrastructure rather than on messing about doing business at micro-level. The scope and depth of direct intervention by the state in microeconomic activities have become much smaller than before. The government nowadays commands a much smaller portion of the available economic resources than before. From 1980 to 1995, the share of government expenditure in GNP declined from 27.2 per cent to 11.7 per cent.

Notwithstanding the downsizing of government's economic role, state intervention has still been active in many areas. As discussed in the previous chapters, China's business environment is characterized by numerous preferential policies. These preferential policies are the vehicle of state intervention. They were designed to influence firms' decision on issues such as what to produce, how to produce, where to produce and for whom to produce.

The Preferential Policies at the Crossroads

As shown in Chapter 2, the investor-oriented preferential policies are partially a legacy of the pre-reform system. In the post-reform period, these policies exist for various reasons. Some privileges for state-owned enterprises are/ were transitional arrangements in a period of rapid economic restructuring while others could be products of rent seeking by bureaucrats and management. A few ad hoc privileges used to serve as instruments to experiment with new reforms. The preferential treatment of foreign investors generally reflects China's efforts to woo foreign capital at a time when the domestic market had yet to have a level playing field for all firms.

In Chapter 3, we observed that the region-oriented preferential policies arose from the experimental nature of China's early reform programmes. The special economic zones started as the "vanguards of reform" to increase the chances of success and to shield the reformers against political risks. After the initial taste of success in the SEZs, the reform-minded leaders went ahead to open up more coastal cities. They relied for the success of the opening up policy on the better infrastructure and industrial potentials of these cities. The expansion of preferential benefits to coastal cities on the one hand discounted the privileges enjoyed by the SEZs and on the other hand enlarged the regional disparity between the coastal regions and the hinterland.

The heavy-industry oriented development strategy in the pre-reform period left behind a distorted industrial structure characterized by a bottleneck of consumer good production, energy and raw material supply, and infrastructure facilities. To overcome the bottleneck, the government carried out industry-oriented policies in taxation, fixed capital investment and credit controls. The urgent need for hard currency to import technology and equipment also drove the government to promote exports. These were the two foci of industry-oriented policies described in Chapter 4.

As discussed in the earlier chapters, China's preferential policies have come to the crossroads. The market-oriented reform has become a consensus of the leadership and hence is conducted in a more systematic manner rather than on a trial-and-error basis. There is no more need to use preferential policies to safeguard experimental reforms. Most economic reforms so far have aimed at building a level playing field for doing business by eliminating investor-oriented privileges. The region-oriented preferential policies, too, have fulfilled their historical task in launching the reform and opening up process into orbit. Maintaining the coastal-region-biased policies would not contribute to social stability in the post-Deng era but could be politically costly to Beijing.

By 1995, China had quadrupled the level of gross national product over that of 1980, five years ahead of the schedule set by the 20-year plan (1981–2000) promulgated in 1982. This achievement marked the end of a historical stage in China's economic development. At this juncture, the Chinese policy-makers had turned their eyes toward new directions of state intervention.

6.2 PROSPECTS OF STATE INTERVENTION IN THE NEW CENTURY

Targets for the Year 2010

In March 1996, China's Eighth National People's Congress approved at its fourth session the *Outlines of the Ninth Five-Year Plan for National Economic and Social Development and the Long-term Target for the Year 2010*[2] [hereafter referred to as the "Outline"]. This landmark document defines the new directions of state intervention and provides a blueprint of national development into the new century [see Table A2.1 (III)].

The "Outline" sets the objectives for the year 2010 as follows:

1. GDP to be double the year 2000 figure;
2. Control population within 1.4 billion and enable people to lead an "even more comfortable life";
3. Establish "a relatively complete socialist market economy", a sounder macroeconomic control system with better agility and effectiveness, and a regulatory framework more in compliance with the rule of law;
4. Establish a modern enterprise system for state-owned enterprises and develop a number of internationally competitive large enterprises and business groups;
5. Optimize industrial structure by:
   – enhancing commercialization and specialization in agriculture;
   – building up a group of national infrastructure projects (including the major water control projects in the Yangtze River and Yellow River such as the "Three Gorges" project) and matching development of infrastructure and basic industries to national economic growth;
   – promoting pillar industries and making them the major driving force of economic growth;
   – increasing markedly the proportion of the tertiary sector in the national economy and its service functions;

6. Promote a more coordinated development of regional economies and gradually narrow the gap in development between different regions.

These objectives confirm our earlier observation that industry policies have become the tone of state intervention toward business. They also indicate a move away from the regional policies that favour the coastal areas. What is noteworthy in these objectives is the emphasis on institution building for a market economy and the development of the so-called "pillar industries". These objectives can be better understood if we look at the development strategies recommended by the document.

Two Transitions

According to the "Outline", to ensure sustainable and rapid economic growth, the key requirement is to achieve two fundamental transitions. One is the transition from the centrally planned economy to a "socialist market economy", in which the market plays a fundamental role in resource allocation under state macro-control. The other is the transition from an extensive growth mode, which is driven by expansion of production inputs, to an intensive growth mode, which is driven by increasing efficiency and productivity.

The first transition obviously forms the foundation for the second transition since firms' instinct to survive in a competitive market is the best guarantee for efficiency. Therefore the document specifies the main foci of market-oriented reforms in the period of the Ninth Five-Year Plan (1996–2000). The foremost task is to restructure the state-owned enterprises into a modern enterprise system. In such a system, enterprises' rights and responsibilities should be clearly defined while government administration must be separated from enterprise management. For this purpose, a legal person asset system and a state asset investor system are to be introduced. The document also pledges to give greater play to the role of the market mechanism in more areas and to further perfect institutions of wholesale markets and factor markets. The emphasis is on the establishment of a procedure for market transactions that is "open, fair and just".

As for the second transition, the "Outline" redefines the scope of state intervention in promoting economic efficiency. Apart from macroeconomic control, the major economic functions of the government are to provide infrastructure and to create and maintain a good business environment. The government also promotes the optimization of the economic structure through implementing industrial policies, regional plans and investment policies.

The document classifies investment projects into three types, namely the "projects of a competition nature", the "projects of a foundation nature", and the projects of a public welfare nature". In the "competitive industries", resources should be allocated primarily by the market. The investment projects in these industries are categorized accordingly as "projects of a competition nature", which should be funded mainly by enterprises and financed through the market. The government, however, will selectively give support to key projects of pillar industries and to high-tech development projects. The pillar industries defined in this document are industries of machinery, electronics, petrochemical, automobile and construction. For these industries, the government may even play a role in "optimizing industrial organizations" to promote economies of scale by coordinating business regrouping among large enterprises or enterprise groups.

The state will continue to play a leading role in "non-competitive industries". The government should be the main fund provider or the leading fundraiser for the "projects of a foundation nature". These projects are likely to be related to infrastructure or "basic industry" (energy supplies and raw materials). Governments "at various levels" should be responsible for funding the "projects of public welfare nature".

6.3 THE FUTURE OF PREFERENTIAL POLICIES

The Ninth Five-Year Plan (1996–2000) outlines more detailed measures to carry out the two transitions discussed above. These measures have important implications for the future of preferential policies.

Future of Investor-Oriented Policies

On the one hand, the Plan vowed to establish a socialist market economy, which is "unified, open, competitive, and integrated in an orderly way", based on fair competition. This goal is consistent with the tax reforms since 1994 that aim to create a level playing field for all enterprises regardless of their ownership. The introduction of a legal person asset system and a state asset investor system is a sure step toward a harder budget constraint on the state-owned enterprises. The Plan also made a commitment to gradually unifying the policies toward domestic enterprises and foreign-funded enterprises and to giving foreign investors national treatment.

On the other hand, however, different approaches will apply to the state-owned enterprises according to their sizes and importance to the state. For small enterprises, a liberalization approach is to apply. The government allows a variety of measures to restructure them, including joint venture, share holding, leasing, contract operation and sales. For the large and medium-sized enterprises, the government is to play a more active role in winner picking. The government pledged to conduct the restructure of asset and management for 1,000 large state enterprises and corporations during the Ninth Five-Year Plan period. According to the Plan, the process entails:

- Selecting the efficient and competent enterprises and giving them support to ensure the survival of the fittest;
- Developing mechanisms whereby the inefficient enterprises may be merged with others or go bankrupt or become downsized for better efficiency;
- Upgrading a selected number of large enterprises and corporations to become giant international corporations;
- Restructuring and merging a selected number of enterprises into large business groups to reap economies of scale so that they can play their full roles as backbone enterprises in the national economy.[3]

As part of the efforts to maintain the "socialist course" of the economic system, these measures aim to keep the state-owned enterprises as the mainstay of the basic industries and even of the "pillar industries".

It is nevertheless difficult to impose financial discipline on enterprises on the one hand while being actively involved in winner picking. As pointed out by the World Bank (1996), the key problem with direct government involvement in enterprise restructuring is the difficulty of picking winners based on past performance. Variation in performance among firms in a transitional economy is much greater than that in an established market economy. Neither the past performance of a firm nor its inherited debt structure is a good guide to future viability.

The official guideline for the so-called "asset structure optimization" programme for the large and medium-sized SOEs includes the measures to:

- Increase capital injection and reduce arrears;
- Reduce staff and improve efficiency;
- Let insolvent enterprises be merged or go bankrupt;
- Divert the over-employed staff to newly created jobs.[4]

For fear that the domino effect of widespread bankruptcy might cause the collapse of the state sector, the focus of the government's intervention has been on rescuing these SOEs rather than allowing them to go bust. The risk of such a policy is obvious.

Injection of state funds to clear arrears may thwart the efforts to impose financial discipline on firms. Some profitable enterprises were compelled by the government authorities to merge with chronically insolvent enterprises.[5] These administratively arranged mergers may jeopordize the financial health of the state-owned enterprises that have so far kept fit in market competition. For the smaller state enterprises, the sale and leasing programmes also carry the risks of being downgraded into insiders' buyouts. The experience in Russia and other transitional economies indicates that privatization programmes through insiders' buyouts tend to be inefficient.[6]

The goal to keep the state-owned enterprises afloat as the "mainstay of the economy" is inherently inconsistent with the goal to build a level playing field for all enterprises. Without a strong governmental commitment to stay away from bailing out the state-owned enterprises, there remains an unsolved problem of balancing between these two contradictory goals. The practice so far suggests that it is much more difficult to remove the preferential policies toward state-owned enterprises than to get rid of the ones toward foreign-funded enterprises.

Future of Industry-Oriented Policies

It is obvious that since China promulgated the first explicit industrial policy in 1989, industry-oriented policies have become the core of China's state intervention. The most remarkable change in these policies is the recent emphasis on the development of "pillar industries". The "pillar industry" strategy is set to overwhelm the earlier strategy that emphasizes development of infrastructure and "basic industries".

The "pillar industry" strategy is particular alluring to Beijing given China's interventionist tradition and the successful stories of active industrial policies practised in the neighbouring Asian high-growth economies, such as Japan, Korea, Singapore and Malaysia. In some high-tech areas, such as satellite launch and bioengineering research, China does have her competitive edge and potential.

The projected progressive inversion of the population's age pyramid under China's one-couple-one-child population policy may also have contributed to the decision to move to high-tech and capital-intensive development mode. According to official estimates, the proportion of the population aged over 65 years old was 5.6 per cent in 1990 but will increase to 10 per cent by the year 2000. The proportion will continue to rise to 25 per cent by 2050.[7]

On the other hand, however, as the world's most populous country with 1.2 billion people, China still possesses the comparative advantages of abundant labour resources. From 1982 to 1990, the working age population (aged between 15 and 64 years old) increased at an annual rate of 2.56 per cent. This was much higher than the annual growth rate of the total population (1.48 per cent). The proportion of the working age population in the total population in 1990 was 66.7 per cent, much higher than the then average figure for the developing countries (60.0 per cent).

It was projected that the annual growth rate of the working age population in the 1990s would be half as fast as that in the 1980s. Still there is excess labour supply in the 1990s. In the early 1990s, the annual unemployed urban residents amounted to 3 to 4 million. About 15 per cent of staff in the large and medium-sized state-owned enterprises were not productively employed. For staff in the state sector, their effective working hours only accounted for 50–70 per cent of total working hours. In the rural area, 40 per cent of the labour force was under-employed or unemployed, amounting to 110 million.[8]

In fact, the Chinese government's rush toward capital-intensive, high-technology development has already met criticisms from some well-known Chinese economists. Lin et al. (1996), for instance, advocate an urgent need to shift development strategy from the heavy-industry oriented one to a "comparative advantage development strategy", which would fully utilize China's abundant labour resources.

Another senior economist, Fan Gang, argues that the shortest way for China to achieve industrialization is to make better use of the labour resources to attract foreign capital and technology. Given China's big population and relatively low per capita possession of natural resources, it is unrealistic for China to develop capital-intensive industries. He warns that government regulations granting approval only to large-scale investment projects would lead to the uneven and inefficient distribution of limited funds. The high-tech, capital-intensive development strategy would "sacrifice the Chinese people for technology". It would reduce job opportunities and sharpen income disparities and social divisions with a minority of highly paid jobs concentrated in a few sectors and business groups.[9]

Apart from the risk of being a pre-matured rush, the "pillar industry" strategy could also become an excuse for state-owned enterprises to seek protection or subsidies from the winner-picking government. Here, the policy-makers in Beijing should be fully aware of the lessons of failed industrial policies practised in some underdeveloped countries. Even for the relatively successful cases like South Korea, any policy imitator should be cautious about the social costs highlighted in the recent political–economic scandals related to government-supported large corporations.[10]

Future of region-oriented policies

The Ninth Five-Year Plan emphasized "a more coordinated development of regional economies" and vowed to gradually narrow the gap in development between different regions. This guideline presents a reversal of the 1980s' policies that favoured coastal regions.

Table 6.1 The Seven Economic Zones

Zones	Advantages	Direction
The Yangtze River Delta and Rivering Zones (with large and medium-sized cities along the Yangtze River as its backbone)	River–sea link, a well-developed agriculture, solid industrial foundation and technology advantages	A comprehensive economic belt
The Bohai Sphere Zone (Liaodong Peninsular, Shandong Peninsular, Beijing, Tianjin and Hebei Province)	A well-developed transportation system, concentration of large cities, poly-technical human capital, and rich coal, iron and oil resources	A comprehensive economic sphere
The Southeast Coastal Zone (Zhujiang River Delta, Southeastern Fujian Province)	Proximity to Hong Kong, Macao and Taiwan; openness to foreign investors	An export-oriented economic zone
Southwest and Southern Provinces (The provinces of Guangxi, Yunan, and west Sichuan Province)	Sea, river and border access, rich agricultural, forestry, water, mineral and tourism resources, and capital assets of national defence industries	An important production base for energy supply, non-ferrous metals, phosphorus and sulphur, tropical and subtropical agricultural goods, and a tourism resort

Table 6.1 Continued

Zones	Advantages	Direction
The Northeastern Zone (The provinces of Heilongjiang, Jilin, and some parts of Inner Mongolia and Liaoning Province)	A well-developed transportation system, a complete system of heavy and chemical industries, abundant land and energy resources	An important base for heavy and chemical industries and an agricultural base
The Five-Central-Province Zone (The provinces of Henan, Hubei, Hunan, Guizhou, Jiangxi)	A fairly sound industrial foundation, convenient transportation with major railway trunk lines passing through	A new economic belt with important agricultural, raw material and machinery industrial bases
The Northwestern Zone (The provinces of Gansu, Shanxi, Shaanxi, Ningxia, Qinghai, Xinjiang, Tibet and part of Inner Mongolia)	Connections with East and Central Asia, rich in agricultural, animal husbandry, energy and mineral resources, well-developed military enterprises	The nation's base for cotton and livestock products, the petrochemical industry, and production of energy and non-ferrous metals

Source: The Ninth Five-Year Plan, *People's Daily*, Beijing, 20 March 1996.

The gist of the "coordinated regional development strategy" is to promote the inter-region division of labour and avoid the overlapping of regional industrial structure. According to the Plan, the state will foster the formation of seven economic zones based on the existing industrial locations and transportation trunk lines (see Table 6.1).

Gradually reducing inter-regional development gaps is another aspect of the "coordinated regional development strategy". Several measures were proposed by the Plan to achieve this:

- The state investment planning will give priority to resource-extraction and infrastructure projects in central and west China. State investment will be the main source of capital funds in major trans-regional infrastructure projects. The state will guide resource-processing and

labour-intensive manufacturing industries to be relocated into central and west China.
- The central government will improve terms of trade for central and west China by adjusting prices of resource-related products.
- The central government will implement an inter-regional fiscal revenue transfer system to redistribute financial resources in favour of central and west China.
- The state will accelerate the pace of reform and opening up in central and west China and guide more foreign investors to the hinterland.
- The state will make greater efforts to support impoverished areas and assist economic progress in areas inhabited by the aborigines.
- The central government will encourage and strengthen economic association, joint venture projects, and technological cooperation between the eastern coastal region and the hinterland. The state will encourage investment in central and west China and promote labour mobility from the hinterland to the eastern coastal region.

As for the status of the special economic zones (SEZs), the Plan repeated the assurance that the basic policies toward the SEZs and Shanghai Pudong New District would stay unchanged. It was, however, pointed out that substantive measures regarding these zones must be adjusted and improved and the SEZ should create their new advantages and advance to a new level. The coastal open zones and open cities were also urged to promote economic development in central and west China.

A major obstacle to achieving a coordinated regional development and efficient inter-regional resource allocation is the rise of regional protectionism. China has tens of thousands of randomly located small-scale state firms that possess limited production capacity. Their survival relies on the usually illegal protectionist policies adopted by their local or regional government authorities. As pointed out by official media, "prompted by self-interest, some regions have blocked the inflow of competitive products from other areas and prohibited the outflow of resources in great need in other areas".[11] Such regional protectionism fosters a large number of inefficient small-scale enterprises, of which the consumption of capital and other resources restrained the growth of potentially more vigorous large-scale enterprises. Based on a survey of 10,000 state-owned enterprises, the China Economic and Analysis Centre under the State Statistics Bureau pointed out that "regional competition within China is far more intense than on the international market". The competition, however, is "not the healthy competition of a free market". The small-scale production sheltered by regional protectionist policies is one of the major causes of business losses in the SOEs. In 1996 these losses amounted to Rmb 61.6 billion and 43.7 per cent of total SOEs were in the red.[12]

The WTO Effect

After about eight years of tenacious efforts, China is finally about to become the World Trade Organization's most populous member. As the world's eleventh largest trading country and the top third-world host country of FDI by the mid-1990s, China will boost its role in the international community with its new membership of the WTO.

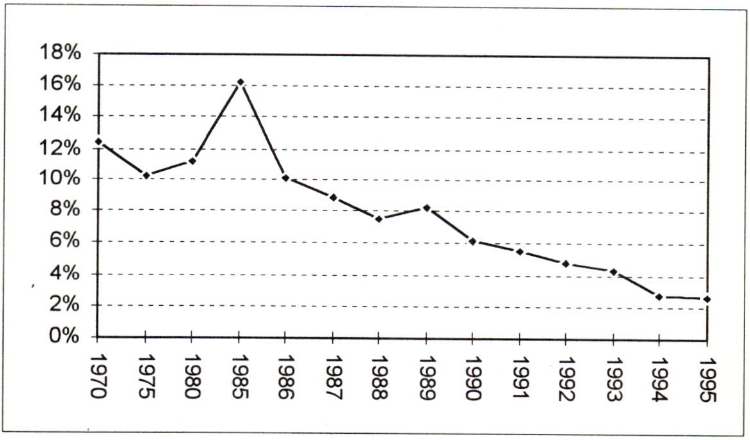

Source: China Statistical Yearbook 1996.

Chart 6.1 Change of China's Effective Tariff Rate

In recent years, China has taken concrete steps to prepare for WTO membership. As observed by Wang (1994), China has undertaken three measures to minimize the shock to domestic industries brought by the GATT–WTO membership. The first measure is to gradually increase the openness of domestic market to prepare the domestic firms for foreign competition. As shown in Chart 6.1, China has gradually reduced the effective tariff rate (defined as the ratio between tariff revenue and total import value) over a period of years. By 1994, China had cut tariff rates for more than 3,500 imports and made export-and-import trade more competitive by issuing more licences to domestic firms.[13] In 1994, China also unified the exchange rates and made *renminbi* (Rmb) convertible for trade and tourism.

The second measure China has taken is to restructure domestic enterprises to make them more competitive in international markets.

Although the overall situation of China's state sector remains gloomy, there have emerged a number of large state corporations that are internationally competitive. The weight of manufactured products (machinery and transport equipment in particular) in exports has risen significantly and these have become the major components of exports. Chart 6.2 shows that the weight of manufactured goods increased from 49.44 per cent in 1985 to 74.41 per cent in 1990 and further increased to 85.56 per cent in 1995. Meanwhile, the weight of machinery and transport equipment rose from 2.82 per cent in 1985 to 9.00 per cent in 1990 and up to 21.10 per cent in 1995. This trend displays the increasing competitiveness of China's industry.

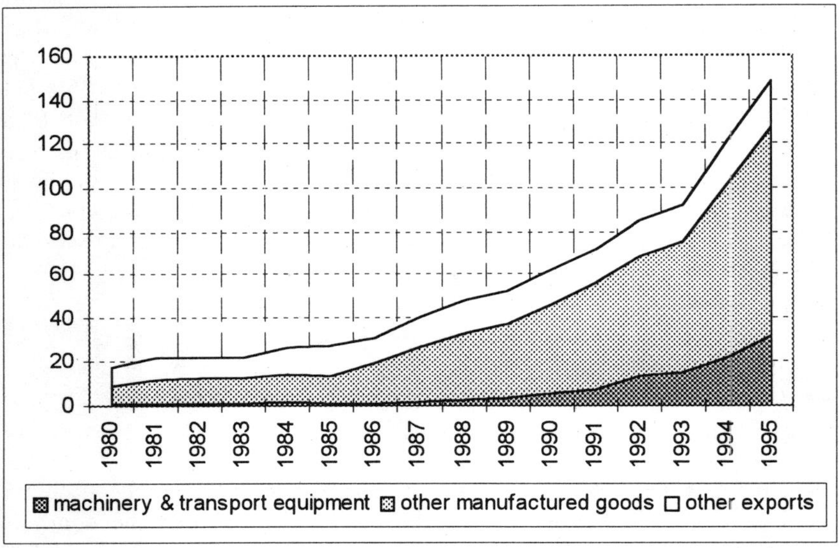

Source: *China Statistical Yearbook 1996.*

Chart 6.2 China's Export Structure (in US$ billion)

The third measure to reduce the shock is to negotiate for ad hoc temporary protections for China's "infant industries" as part of the conditions to join the WTO. Meanwhile China has used industrial policies to systematically guide foreign investment into the pillar industries such as electronics and car-manufacturing (see Chapter 4).

WTO membership will certainly have a significant impact on China's state intervention and the system of preferential policies. On the benefit side, the membership will ease needless tensions between China and her major trading partners, such as the US. Many trade disputes could be resolved through WTO mechanisms rather by direct clashes. On the side of responsibilities, the WTO rules require that foreign investment and trade be conducted on fair-play commercial terms, with no subsidies to exports or restrictions on imports. As a WTO member, China also has to honour intellectual property rights and drop a variety of restrictions on foreign investors. All these will reduce the scope for manoeuvre of state interventionist policy.

One effect is that protectionist policies against foreign competition must be circumvented if not fully abandoned. Since 1989, China, as a founding member of Asia-Pacific Economic Cooperation (APEC), has made some important "down-payments" for free trade. In April 1992, China cancelled all import adjustment taxes. On 31 December 1993, China lowered the arithmetical average level of tariff rate from 39.9 per cent down to 36.4 per cent by reducing import tariffs on 2,998 items.[14] From 1994 to 1996, China cut average tariff rates from 35.9 per cent down to 23 per cent. China also pledged to slash the tariffs for more than 4,000 items out of 6,000 imported goods by at least 30 per cent from 1996. This would lower import tariffs further down to an average of 15 per cent by the end of 1997. On top of that, China is to lift 170 import quotas and to permit the setting up of Sino–foreign trading companies.[15]

Another effect is that China must be more committed to practising the principle of national treatment to foreign investors. To buy entry into the WTO, China has agreed to open import-and-export business to foreign-funded firms within three years after her entry and to remove all import quotas within 12 years.[16] In the areas that have so far been closed to foreign investors, such as the telecommunications sector, China will surely encounter greater pressure from the international community to open the domestic market. Meanwhile, to meet the WTO rules, China must first make her subsidies to the state enterprises explicit and transparent and then pledge to remove them in the longer term.

In the field of industrial policies, China has to adapt the pillar-industry strategy to standards acceptable to the WTO. One can expect this front to be the vulnerable part of China's future relationship with the WTO.

Entering into the new century, the role of China's state intervention will be defined less by the Chinese government and more by the interactions between China on the one side and the foreign countries and international organizations on the other side. With the globalization of national economies, this trend of international interdependence regarding the role of state intervention appears to be inevitable for all nations.

NOTES

1. The "market-friendly" development strategy was proposed by the World Bank in its *World Development Report 1991*. The strategy requires government intervention to be applied only in areas where markets alone cannot be relied upon. The role of the state should ensure a conducive climate for enterprises and market to thrive on.
2. Xinhua News Agency Daily Report, 20 March 1996.
3. Xinhua News Agency Daily Report, 20 March 1996.
4. The 4-point guideline is written in sixteen Chinese charaters, which are: "*zeng zi jian zhai, jian ren zeng xiao, jianbing pochan, fenliu renyuan*".
5. *Yazhou Zhoukan* [The International Chinese Weekly], 24–30 March 1997, p. 30.
6. World Bank (1996), pp. 54–56.
7. AFP, Reuter, *Straits Times,* Singapore, 25 November 1996.
8. Ma and Fang eds (1993), pp. 19–24.
9. *China Daily,* Beijing, 9 May 1996.
10. For instance, a major loan scandal occurred in January 1997 rocking the Korean financial market, in which the Hanbo Group went bankrupt. The group, being the fourteenth largest conglomerate in South Korea, was accused of using government links to obtain massive loans worth 20 times the group's net assets (AFP, *Straits Times,* Singapore, 1 February 1997).
11. A commentary in *China Daily,* Beijing, 19 December 1996.
12. AFP, *Straits Times,* Singapore, 28 January 1997.
13. Wang (1994), p. 202.
14. Sino–US Information Inc. (1995), p. 175.
15. APEC (1995).
16. *Yazhou Zhoukan* [The International Chinese Weekly], 17–23 March 1997, p. 10.

Appendix 1. Preferential Tax Policies

Table A.1.1 Changes in Preferential Tax Policies (1994–96)

Previous policies	New policies
Exemption from Import Duty and VAT on • Import of reasonable amount of vehicles and office equipment for own use of foreign-funded enterprises[1] • Import of reasonable amount of vehicles and office equipment for own use of enterprises, institutions and other organizations in Special Economic Zones, Economic and Technological Development Zones and Bonded Areas	No exemption from Import Duty and VAT on • vehicles (automobiles and motor cycles), except those with tax exemption according to inter-government agreement, or those presented by international organization or foreign government, from 4 July 1994 • office equipment, except those with tax exemption according to inter-government agreement, or those presented by international organization or foreign government, from 1 January 1995
Exemption from Import Duty and VAT on: Import of machinery and equipment, their parts and other materials required for installation by equity joint ventures and wholly foreign-owned enterprises, using their "total investment" fund, (i.e. registered capital plus planned bank loans for the enterprise in qestion) or approved amount of additional "total investment" fund	No such tax exemption for foreign-funded enterprises set up after 1 April 1996 • Grace period for foreign-funded enterprises set up between 1 October 1995 and 1 April 1996: the tax exemption period would be extended until 30 June 1997 for foreign-funded enterprises with the "total investment fund" less than $US 30 million, or until 30 June 1998 for foreign-funded enterprises with the "total investment fund" equal to or larger than $US 30 million

Table A.1.1 Continued

Previous policies	New policies
Exemption from Import Duty and VAT on • Import of machinery, parts, raw materials, vehicles for infrastructure construction in Special Economic Zones, Pudong New Area, Economic and Technological Development Zones, Bonded Areas, Border Economic Cooperation Zones and State Holiday Resort Zones • Import of machinery, parts, raw materials, fuel for enterprises in Special Economic Zones, Economic and Technological Development Zones and Bonded Areas, foreign-funded enterprises in Coastal or Inland Open Cities	The amount of duty-free imports of Special Economic Zones and Pudong New Area would be subject to a quota from July 1995, the size of the quota would be reduced by 20% each year until year 2000 when the tax exemption is to be eliminated (Singapore–China Suzhou Industrial Park was also granted with the same transitional benefits in 1996) • No tax exemption in open zones except Special Economic Zones, and Pudong New Area from 1 April 1996 • No tax exemption on import of automobiles and motor cycles from 4 July 1994 • No tax exemption on import of 20 commodities[2] from 1 January 1995
Half duties on import of commodities to be sold within Special Economic Zones, up to the approved amount, half VAT on oil, cigarettes and wine, exemption from VAT for other imported commodities sold within Special Economic Zone.	No half duties and exemption from VAT on import of commodities to be sold within Special Economic Zones from 1 January 1996
Half duties and VAT on sale of goods from barter trade, or from investors of neighbouring countries as a part of their investment in Border Open Cities	No tax exemption on sale of goods from barter trade, or from investors of neighbouring countries in Border Open Cities from 1 April 1996

Table A.1.1 Continued

Previous policies	New policies
Exemption from Import Duty and VAT on: (1) Import of equipment, instrument and other materials for technological renovation, which have no domestic supplies, for • Coastal Open Cities and Coastal Open Economic Zones (until end of 1993, then half duty until end of 1995) • Inland Open Cities and Border Open Cities (until end of 1995) • high-tech enterprises in High-Tech Industrial Development Zones (2) Import of equipment, instrument and other materials for export-oriented agriculture in • Coastal Open Economic Zones (until end of 1993, then half duty until end of 1995), • Border Open Cities and Inland Open Cities (until end of 1995) (3) Import of equipment and raw materials for compensation trade	No tax exemption from 1 April 1996

Notes:

1. Office equipment includes: (1) office machines and tools (e.g. typewriter, photocopier, micro-computer, fax machine etc.); (2) paper and stationery; (3) document-storing facilities (e.g. safe, filing cabinet); (4) office furniture and electrical equipment (e.g. refrigerator, air-conditioner, TV set, etc.).
2. The 20 commodities include TV set, video camera, video recorder, video player, audio equipment, air-conditioner, refrigerator, washing machine, camera, photocopier, SPC telephone exchanger, micro-computer, telephone, radio paging system, fax machine, calculator, typewriter and word processor, furniture, lamp, food and drink).

Source:

China's Customs, Beijing, 1994, no.7; *Gazette of Ministry of Foreign Trade and Economic Cooperation of the PRC,*Beijing: MOFTEC, 1995; *International Business* Beijing, various issues; *International Trade News,* Beijing, various issues; *China Daily,* Beijing, 2 February 1997.

Table A.1.2 Changes in Export Rebate Rates

Date	Changes in Export Rebate Rates
1 January 1994 –30 June 1995	New export rebate rates set out in conjunction with the new VAT, business tax and consumption tax • rebate rate of 17% for products attracting a VAT rate of 17% • rebate rate of 13% for products attracting a VAT rate of 13% (e.g., grains, edible oil, chemical fertilizer and farm machinery) • no rebate for crude oil, aids to foreign countries, sugar, and products which are forbidden to be exported • no rebate for products which are purchased by the exporter directly from their producers and bear no VAT when sold to the exporter (e.g. agricultural products sold directly by the farmers which are exempt from VAT) • special rate of 6% for selected products (e.g. handicrafts) which are purchased by the exporter from a "small taxpayer", who has annual sales of less than Rmb 1 million and does not issue VAT invoices; no rebate for other products which are purchased by the exporter from the "small taxpayers" • rebate of the full amount of the consumption tax borne when the products are purchased by the exporter
1 July 1995–31 December 1995	• rebate rate of 3% for coal and agricultural products • rebate rate of 10% for products using agricultural products as raw materials, and other products which attract a VAT rate of 13% • rebate rate of 14% for other products which attract a VAT rate of 17%
1 January 1996	• rebate rate of 3% for coal and agricultural products • rebate rate of 6% for products using agricultural products as raw materials, and other products which attract a VAT rate of 13% • rebate rate of 9% for other products which attract a VAT rate of 17%

Source:
"Measures For Export Rebates and Tax Exemption" in *Gazette of Ministry of Foreign Trade and Economic Cooperation of the PRC*, Beijing: MOFTEC, 1994, no. 19; "State Council Notice on Reduction of Export Rebate Rate and Enhanced Administration on Export Tax Rebate" in *Gazette of Ministry of Foreign Trade and Economic Cooperation of the PRC*, Beijing: MOFTEC, 1995.

Table A.1.3 Major Preferential Tax Policies Still Applicable to Foreign Investors (1996–97)

Categories	Preferential policies
Special rate of national corporate income tax	(1) 15% for • All foreign-funded enterprises (including those in service sector) in Special Economic Zones • All "Production-Oriented" (i.e. non-service) foreign-funded enterprises in Economic and Technological Development Zones, Pudong New Area, Bonded Area. • Selected foreign-funded enterprises in Coastal Open Cities, Inland Open Cities and Coastal Open Economic Zone which are technology intensive, or with foreign investment more than US$ 30 million, or are energy or transportation projects • High-Tech enterprises in High-Tech Industrial Development Zone • Equity joint ventures in construction of ports or docks • Foreign-funded banks, with foreign capital more than US$ 10 million, and with an operation period of more than 10 years. (2) 24% for • "Production-Oriented" (i.e., non-service) foreign-funded enterprises in Coastal Open Cities, Inland Open Cities, Coastal Open Economic Zone. • All foreign-funded enterprises in Border Open Cities, Border Economic Cooperation Zones and State Holiday Resort Zones

Table A.1.3 Continued

Categories	Preferential policies
Tax holidays for corporate income tax	• "Production-Oriented" (i.e. non-service) foreign-funded enterprises (but excluding those engaged in exploitation of oil, gas, rare or precious metals), with an operation period of more than 10 years, will from the first year they make profit, be exempt from paying the tax for two years and will pay only half of the tax for the following three years • After the above exemption and reduction period, "export-oriented" foreign-funded enterprises (with their annual value of exports more than 70% of the value of their annual products) will pay half of the tax (not less than 10%), "technologically advanced foreign-funded enterprises" will pay half of the tax (not less than 10%) for three more years • After the above exemption and reduction period (paragraph 1), foreign-funded enterprises engaged in agriculture, forestry or animal husbandry, or those located in remote or economically under-developed areas will pay the national at the reduced rate of between 15–30% for 10 more years • Equity joint ventures engaged in construction of ports or docks, with an operation period for more than 10 years, will from the first year they make profit, be exempt from paying the tax for five years and will pay only half of the tax for the following five years • Foreign-funded banks, with foreign capital more than US$ 10 million, and with an operation period for more than 10 years, will from the first year they make profit, be exempt from paying the tax for one year and will pay only half of the tax for the following two years • Foreign-funded enterprises in service sector of Special Economic Zones, with foreign investment more than US$ 5 million, and with an operation period for more than 10 years, will from the first year they make profit, be exempt from paying the tax for one year and will pay only half of the tax for the following two years • Foreign-funded enterprises in infrastructure or agriculture sectors in Special Economic Zones, energy or transportation sector in Pudong New Area, with an operation period of more than 15 years, will from the first year they make profit, be exempt from paying the tax for five years and will pay only half of the tax for the following five years

Table A.1.3 Continued

Categories	Preferential policies
Rebate of corporate income tax for reinvestment	• 40% rebate of tax paid, if profit is reinvested for more than five years • 100% rebate of tax paid, if profit is reinvested in "export-oriented" or "technologically advanced enterprises", for more than five years • 100% rebate of tax paid, if profit is reinvested in infrastructure and agriculture in Hainan Special Economic Zone, for more than five years
Withholding tax	• exemption on dividend from foreign-funded enterprises • exemption on interest on loans provided by international financial organizations, or loans with preferential terms • 10% or 0% on royalties for technology transfer in agriculture, scientific research, energy, transportation, energy and environment conservation, and special technology in selected key areas • 10% or less on dividends, rent, interest rate and royalties etc. in Special Economic Zones, Economic and Technological Development Zones, and Coastal and Inland Open Cities
Personal income tax	• an extra deduction of Rmb 3,200 per month • exemption from tax on approved subsidies, and dividends for foreign-funded enterprises
VAT and other turnover tax	• rebate for foreign-funded enterprises set up before 31 December 1993, on the extra amount of VAT, business tax of consumption tax paid, compared with the tax liable under the old "Consolidated Industrial and Commercial Tax" system, for a period up to five years • exemption from business tax of foreign banks for five years from the day when they start business

Table A.1.3 ***Continued***

Categories	Preferential policies
Import duties and VAT on imports	Exemption from Import Duty and VAT on • import of machinery as part of the pledged capital of the foreign investors by equity joint ventures, wholly foreign-owned enterprises, or contribution by the foreign partners using the foreign fund by the cooperative joint ventures, subject to further clarification • import of machinery using the "total investment fund" by equity joint ventures, wholly foreign-owned enterprises set up before 1 April 1996, until 31 December 1996 for those with "total investment fund" less than US$30 million, or 31 December 1997 for those with "total investment fund" equal to or larger than US $30 million • import of machinery used for exploration of off-shore petroleum by cooperative joint ventures, and import of machinery using the foreign fund (as contribution of the foreign partner) by the cooperative joint ventures in selected sectors, subject to further clarification • import of raw materials, parts, components, etc. of all foreign-funded enterprises for export processing
Export duties and VAT rebate on exports	• exemption from Export Duty and VAT (on value added by the exporting firms) for export goods produced by themselves, excluding oil and some specific products, by all foreign-funded enterprises • full VAT rebate (including purchases VAT) for export goods, excluding oil and some specific products, by foreign-funded enterprises set up after 1 January 1994
Other taxes	• exemption from coordination tax for directions of fixed capital investment and urban maintenance and development tax for all foreign-funded enterprises

Source: APEC, Committee for Trade and Industry (1994); State Taxation Bureau (1994, 1995, 1996); Zhang, X. ed. (1995).

Table A1.4 Regional Differences in Corporate Income Tax

Enterprises in the Nation	Enterprises in SEZs and Other Open Zones
Rate of national tax: (1) 30% national tax for ordinary enterprises (2) 15% national tax for foreign equity joint ventures in construction of ports or docks (3) 15% national tax: for foreign-funded banks, with foreign capital more than US$ 10 million, and with an operation period for more than 10 years	Rate of national tax: (1) 15% national tax for • All foreign-funded enterprises and domestic enterprises in SEZs • All "Production-Oriented" (i.e. non-service) foreign-funded enterprises in Economic and Technological Development Zones, Pudong New Area, and Bonded Areas • Selected foreign-funded enterprises in Coastal Open Cities, Inland Open Cities and Coastal Economic Open Zones which are technology intensive, or with foreign investment more than US$ 30 million, or in infrastructure construction of energy or transportation projects • High-tech enterprises in High-Tech Industry Development Zones (2) 24% national tax for • "Production-Oriented" (i.e. non-service) foreign-funded enterprises in Coastal Open Cities, Inland Open Cities, and Coastal Economic Open Zones All foreign-funded enterprises in Border Open Cities, Border Economic Cooperation Zones and State Holiday Resort Zones, and domestic enterprises in Border Economic Cooperation Zones

Table A1.4 Continued

Enterprises in the Nation	Enterprises in SEZs and Other Open Zones
Exemption from or reduction of the national tax: (1) "Production-oriented" (i.e. non-service) foreign-funded enterprises (excluding those engaged in exploitation of oil, gas, rare or precious metals), with an operation period of more than 10 years, will, from the first year they make profit, be exempt from paying the tax for two years and will pay only half of the tax for the following three years (2) After the exemption and reduction period in paragraph (1), "export-oriented" foreign-funded enterprises (with their annual value of exports more than 70% of the value of their annual products) will pay half of the tax (not less than 10%), "technologically advanced foreign-funded enterprises" will pay half of the tax (not less than 10%) for another three years (3) After the exemption and reduction period in paragraph 1, foreign-funded enterprises engaged in agriculture, forestry or animal husbandry, or those located in remote or economically under-developed areas will pay the national tax at the reduced rate between 15–30% for another 10 years (4) Equity joint ventures engaged in construction of ports or docks, with an operation period of more than 10 years, will, from the first year they make profit, be exempt from paying the tax for five years and will pay only half of the tax for the following five years (5) Foreign-funded banks, with foreign capital more than US$ 10 million, and with an operation period of more than 10 years, will, from the first year they make profit, be exempt from paying the tax for one year and will pay only half of the tax for the following two years	Exemption from or reduction of the national tax: (1) Foreign-funded enterprises in the service sector of SEZs, with foreign investment more than US$ 5 million, and with an operation period of more than 10 years, will from the first year they make profit, be exempt from paying the tax for one year and will pay only half of the tax for the following two years. (2) Foreign-funded enterprises in infrastructure construction or agriculture of SEZs, infrastructure construction of energy or transportation projects in Pudong New Area, with an operation period of more than 15 years, will from the first year they make profit, be exempt from paying the tax for five years and will pay only half of the tax for the following five years

Table A1.4 Continued

Enterprises in the Nation	Enterprises In SEZs and Other Open Zones
Rate of local tax: 3 % • Exemption or reduction for foreign-funded enterprises: at the discretion of the local government	Same as the left-hand column
Withholding tax: 20% on dividends, rent, interest rate and royalties, etc. Exemption or reduction: (1) Exemption for dividend from foreign-funded enterprises (2) Exemption for interest on loans provided by international financial organizations, or loans with preferential terms (3) 10% or 0% on royalties for technology transfer in agriculture, scientific research, energy, transportation, energy and environment conservation, and special technology in selected key departments	Withholding tax: 10% or less on dividends, rent, interest rate and royalties, etc. in Special Economic Zones, Economic and Technological Development Zones, and Coastal and Inland Open Cities
Refund for profit reinvestment: (1) 40% refund on tax paid for reinvested profit, if invested for more than five years (2) 100% refund on tax paid for reinvested profit, if invested in "export-oriented" or "technologically advanced enterprises", for more than five years	Refund for profit reinvestment: 100% refund on tax paid for reinvested profit, if invested in infrastructure and agriculture in Hainan SEZ, for more than five years
Loss carried over for up to five years	Same as the left-hand column

Source: APEC, Committee for Trade and Industry (1994); Gao S. ed. (1994); Liu X. et al. eds (1992); State Taxation Bureau (1994, 1995, 1996); State Taxation Bureau and Ministry of Finance (1993); Zhang X. (ed.) (1995).

Table A1.5 Regional Differences in Customs Duty and VAT on Exports and Imports (Up to the End of 1993)

Enterprises in the Nation	Enterprises in SEZs and Other Open Zones
Exemption from Import Duty and VAT on (1) Imports of machinery and equipment, their parts and components and other materials required for construction of sites and factories and installation and reinforcement of the machinery by equity joint ventures and wholly foreign-owned enterprises within the amount of their total approved investment, or that within the amount of approved additional investment where the domestic supply cannot be guaranteed (2) Imports of machinery and equipment, their parts and components and other materials required for construction of sites and factories and installation and reinforcement of the machinery, according to the contract, by cooperative joint ventures in infrastructure construction of energy and transportation projects, manufacturing, agriculture, forestry, animal husbandry, deep sea fishing, scientific research, education, public health and medical care,	Exemption from Import Duty and VAT on (1) Imports of machinery, parts, raw materials, vehicles for infrastructure construction in SEZs, Pudong New Area, Economic and Technological Development Zones, Bonded Areas, Border Economic Cooperation Zones, and State Holiday Resort Zones (2) Imports of machinery, parts, raw materials, fuel by enterprises in SEZs, Economic and Technological Development Zones and Bonded Areas, foreign-funded enterprises in Coastal or Inland Open Cities (3) Imports of reasonable quantity of vehicles and office articles and equipment for own use by enterprises, institutions and other organizations in SEZs, Economic and Technological Development Zones and Bonded Areas (4) Imports of raw materials, parts, components etc. for export by enterprises in SEZs, Economic and Technological Development Zones and Bonded Areas, high-tech enterprises in High-Tech Industry Development Zones

Table A1.5 Continued

Enterprises in the Nation	Enterprises in SEZs and Other Open Zones
but excluding those in commerce, food and beverage, service, employee training, automotive transportation and off-shore fishing etc. (3) Imports of reasonable quantity of vehicles and office articles and equipment for foreign-funded enterprises' own use (4) Imports of raw materials, parts, components etc. by foreign-funded enterprises for exports	(5) Imports of equipment, instrument and other materials for technological renovation, where there is no domestic supply, in Coastal Open Cities and Coastal Economic Open Zones (before 1993), Inland Open Cities and Border Open Cities (before 1996), equipment and instrument for high-tech development where there is no domestic supply for high-tech enterprises in High-Tech Industry Development Zones, equipment, instrument and other materials for export oriented agriculture in Coastal Economic Open Zones (before 1993), Border Open Cities and Inland Open Cities (before 1996)
Reduction of Import Duty and VAT Not applicable	Reduction of Import Duty and VAT (1) Half import duties on imports of commodities to be sold within SEZs, up to the approved amount, half VAT on oil, cigarettes and wine, exemption from VAT for other imported commodities sold in SEZ (2) Half import duties and VAT on sale of goods from barter trade, or from investors of neighbouring countries as a part of their investment in Border Open Cities

Source: Liu X. et al. eds (1992); PRC Customs (1994); State Taxation Bureau and Ministry of Finance (1993).

Appendix 2. Economic Plans

Table A.2.1 China's Long-Term Economic Plans

Title and Period	Date and Event	Main Objectives
Guideline for the Transform-ation Period (1953–1967)	September 1954 First Session of the First National People's Congress	• Lay a solid foundation for socialist industrialization • Transform all sectors into socialist economic sectors
Great Leap Forward Plan (1958–1972)	May 1958 Second Plenary of the Eighth CPC central committee	• Surpass Britain in output volumes of major industrial products • Build a modernized industrial foundation and a modernized agricultural foundation
Ten-Year Plan of National Economic Develop-ment (1976–1985)	Febrary 1978 First Session of the Fifth National People's Congress	• Lay a solid foundation for achieving modernization of industry, agriculture, national defence, and science and technology • Grain output: 400 million tons; steel output: 60 million tons; petroleum output 250 million tons; etc. • Construct 120 major projects in heavy industry and infrastructure • Mechanize 70% of agricultural operations • Build 14 heavy industrial bases

Table A.2.1 Continued

Title and Period	Date and Event	Main Objectives
Twenty-Year Perspective Plan (1981–2000)	September 1982 Twelfth National Congress of the CPC	• Quadruple gross industrial and agricultural product values • Realize a "comfortable" standard of living for the people • Be one of the top countries in terms of total national income and major industrial and agricultural products • Strategic foci: agriculture, energy and transportation, education and science
Ten-Year Plan for National Economic and Social Development (1991–2000)	April 1991 Fourth Session of the Seventh National People's Congress	• GNP to grow at annual rate of 6.0% and reach Rmb 3,110 billion at the price of 1990 • Gross industrial and agricultural product values to grow at annual rate of 6.1% • Realize a "comfortable" standard of living for the people • Adjust industrial structure: strengthen agriculture, basic industries, and infrastructure facilities; restructure and upgrade manufacturing industry; develop electronic industry, construction sector, and the tertiary industry • Improve inter-regional economic structure • Make primary education universal

Table A.2.1 Continued

Title and Period	Date and Event	Main Objectives
Outline of the Long-Term Target for 2010 (1996–2010)	March 1996 Fourth Session of the Eighth National People's Congress	• GDP to be double the year 2000 figure • Control population within 1.4 billion and enable people to lead an even more comfortable life • Establish a relatively complete socialist market economy, a sounder macroeconomic control system with better flexibility and effectiveness, and a regulatory framework more in compliance with rule of law • Establish a modern enterprise system for state-owned enterprises and develop a number of internationally competitive large enterprises and business groups • Optimize industrial structure: – enhance commercialization and specialization in agriculture; – build up a group of national infrastructure projects and match development of infrastructure and basic industries to national economic growth; – promote pillar industries and make them the major driving force of economic growth; – increase markedly the proportion of the tertiary in the national economy and its service functions • Promote a more coordinated development of regional economies and gradually narrow the gap in development between different regions

Source: *Zhongguo Jingji Nianjian* [Almanac of China's Economy], various issues; Zhao (1989); and People's Daily and China Industrial Economic Association (1991); Xinhua News Agency, 20 March 1996.

Table A.2.2 China's Five-Year Economic Plans Before the 1980s

Five-Year Plan	Main Objectives	Remarks
First FYP (1953–1957)	• Build the primary foundation of socialist industrialization by constructing the 156 core heavy-industry projects designed with the help of the Soviet Union and the 694 key construction items • Gross industrial product value to grow at 14.7% per annum • Increase industrial production capacity and output (by 1957 annual output should reach these targets: steel 4,120,000 tons, electricity 15.9 kilowatt hours, coal 113 million tons, cement 6 million tons, etc.) • Start the first stage of "socialist transformation" of agriculture, handicraft sector, and capitalist sector	• The official plan was promulgated in July 1955 • Gross industrial product value grew 18% per annum (at comparable prices) • Completed 68 of the 156 core projects by 1957 • Built a number of new industrial sectors • Collectivized farming and handicraft sectors; transformed most capitalist firms into state-managed enterprises

Table A.2.2 Continued

Five-Year Plan	Main Objectives	Remarks
Second FYP (1958–1962)	• Continue heavy-industry oriented construction and lay a solid foundation for socialist industrialization • Raise standard of living and strengthen national defence • Gross industrial and agricultural product value to increase 75% in five years; gross industrial product value to increase 100% in five years	• The plan was announced in 1956 • The plan was pushed aside during the Great Leap Forward campaign (1958–60) • The Great Leap Foward campaign led to the collapsed of the economy • Economic growth stagnated during the five years
Third FYP (1966–1970)	• Give priority to national defence and military industries • Relocate industries into the inland "third front" areas • Invest Rmb 85 billion in capital construction, of which 42.4% would go to "third front" area and 47% go to industry	• National planning and production were interrupted by the Cultural Revolution • The economy experienced negative growth in 1967 and 1968 • Major efficieny indicators declined although the total social output value grew on average at 9.3% per annum

Table A.2.2 Continued

Five–Year Plan	Main Objectives	Remarks
Fourth FYP (1971–1975)	• Continuet to focus on the construction of "third front" millitary–heavy industrial bases • Industrial annual growth rate to reach 12.8%; steel output to reach 35 to 40 million tons by 1975 • Develop 10 self-sufficient economic regions nationwide • Encourage development of local small-sized industries	• Economic planning was disturbed by political instability • The "cellular economy" structure emerged • Major efficiency indicators continued to decline while the industrial annual growth rate reached 9.3%
Fifth FYP (1976–1980)	• Industrial annual growth rate to reach 10–12% • Focus on agriculture, energy, and raw material sectors to ensure the fulfilment of the Ten-Year Plan of National Economic Development (1976–1985) • Actively seek foreign technologies and capital; introduce 22 sets of foreign equipment worth US$ 13 billion	• Political struggles before and after Mao's death in 1976 delayed the drafting of the plan. The plan was mapped out only in Feburary 1978 • Implementation of the plan overstretched the economy and caused a crisis to the state budget

Source: *Zhongguo Jingji Nianjian* [Almanac of China's Economy], various issues; Zhao (1989); and People's Daily and China Industrial Economic Association (1991).

Table A2.3 Growth and Structural Changes from the First to the Fifth Five-Year Plan (1952–1980)

Period	1st FYP (1953 –57)	2nd FYP (1958 –62)	Retrench-ment (1963–65)	3ird FYP (1966 –70)	4th FYP (1971 –75)	5th FYP (1976 –80)
Total social output value	11.3	–0.4	15.5	9.3	7.3	8.3
Output value of industry and agriculture	10.9	0.6	15.7	9.6	7.8	8.1
Output value of agriculture	4.5	–4.4	11.1	2.9	3.4	3.2
Output value of light industry	12.9	1.1	21.2	8.7	7.9	11.5
Output value of heavy industry	25.4	6.6	14.9	15.0	10.3	8.2
National income	8.9	–3.1	14.7	8.3	5.5	6.1
Rate of accumulation	24.2	30.8	22.7	26.3	33.3	33.2

Note: All figures are average annual growth rates calculated on comparable prices except for "rate of accumulation", which is defined as the proportion of national income that is not used for current year consumption.

Source: *Zhongguo Jinrong Nianjian* [Almanac of China's Finance] 1992, p. 623; *China Statistical Yearbook*, various issues.

Table A2.4 The Sixth Five-Year Plan (1981–85): Targets and Results

Targets	Planned	Results Achieved
Annual Growth Rate of Gross Social Product	4.0%	11.1%
Annual Growth Rate of Agriculture Output Value	4.0%	8.1%
Annual Growth Rate of Industry Output Value	4.0%	12.0%
Annual Growth Rate of Light Industry Output Value	5.0%	13.5%
Annual Growth Rate of Heavy Industry Output Value	3.0%	10.7%
Percentage Ratios of Agriculture, Light Industry, and Heavy Industry in 1985	27.2% 36.0% 36.7%	27.1% 34.3% 38.6%
Annual Growth Rate of National Income	4.0%	10.0%
Accumulation Rate by 1985	29%	35%
Energy Consumption Per Rmb 10,000 Total Industry Output Value by 1985 (Figure for 1980 is 8.15 tons)	7.15 tons standard coal	8.43 tons (based on 1980 prices)
Investment in Capital Construction (based on current prices)	Rmb 230 billion	Rmb 341 billion
In which:		
Energy supply sector	Rmb 58.7 billion (25.5%)	Rmb 69.6 billion (20.4%)
Transportation sector	Rmb 29.9 billion (13.0%)	Rmb 45.4 billion (13.3%)
Investment in Enterprises' Technology Upgrading (based on current prices)	Rmb 130 billion	Rmb 147.5 billion
Increase of Bank Deposits in Urban and Rural Areas (1981–85)	Rmb 63 billion	Rmb 122.3 billion
Annual Growth Rate of Exports (based on current price)	8.1%	8.6%
Annual Growth Rate of Per Capita Consumption	4.1%	9.6%

Note: All growth rates are based on comparable prices except otherwise noted.

Source: *China Statistical Yearbook 1992*, pp. 18–23; *China Statistical Yearbook 1996*, pp. 22–29, various issues.

Table A2.5 The Seventh Five-Year Plan (1986–90): Targets and Results

Targets	Planned	Results Achieved
Annual Growth Rate of Gross Social Product	6.7%	10.4%
Annual Growth Rate of Agriculture Output Value	4.0%	4.8%
Annual Growth Rate of Industry Output Value	7.5%	13.1%
Annual Growth Rate of GNP	7.5%	7.7%
Percentage Output Ratios of Agriculture, Light Industry, and Heavy Industry in 1990	21.0% 39.4% 39.6%	24.3% 37.4% 38.3%
Percentage Output Ratios of Primary, Secondary and Tertiary Industries in 1990	27.4% 47.4% 25.2%	28.4% 43.6% 28.0%
Annual Growth Rate of National Income	6.7%	7.6%
Average Accumulation Rate	30%	34%
Energy Consumption Per Rmb 10,000 National Income by 1990 (figure for 1985 is 12.9 tons based on 1980 prices)	11.4 tons standard coal	11.56 tons (based on 1980 prices)
Investment in Capital Construction (in the state sector, based on current prices)	Rmb 500 billion	Rmb 735.7 billion
In which:		
Energy supply sector	Rmb 117.7 billion (23.5%)	Rmb 202.3 billion (27.5%)
Transportation sector	Rmb 56.8 billion (14.8%)	Rmb 95.6 billion (13.0%)
Investment Technology Upgrading (in the state sector, based on current prices)	Rmb 276 billion	Rmb 397.7 billion
Increase of Bank Credit Sources (1985–90)	Rmb 574.5 billion	Rmb 1046.3 billion
Annual Growth Rate of Exports (based on current prices)	8.1%	17.8%
Annual Growth Rate of Per Capita Resident Consumption	5.0%	2.4%

Note: All growth rates are based on comparable prices except otherwise noted.

Source: *China Statistical Yearbook 1992*, pp. 18–23, 164; *China Statistical Yearbook 1996*, pp. 22–29.

Table A2.6 The Eighth Five-Year Plan (1991–95): Targets and Results

Targets	Planned	Results Achieved
Annual Growth Rate of Agriculture Output Value	3.5%	6.7%
Annual Growth Rate of Industry Output Value	6.5%	22.2%
Annual Growth Rate of Value–added in the Tertiary Industry	9.0%	9.8%
Annual Growth Rate of GNP	6.0%	11.6%
Energy Consumption Per Rmb 10,000 GNP by 1995 (Figure for 1990 is 9.3 tons, based on 1980 prices)	8.5 tons standard coal	6.77 tons (based on 1980 prices)
Total Investment in Fixed Assets (based on current prices)	Rmb 2,600 billion	Rmb 6,381 billion
In which: investment in the state sector	Rmb 1,700 billion	Rmb 4,300 billion
Investment Capital Construction (in the state sector, based on current prices)	Rmb 840 billion	Rmb 2,358 billion
Investment Technology Upgrading (in the state sector, based on current prices)	Rmb 550 billion	Rmb 1,090 billion
Annual Increase of Bank Credit Size (based on current prices)	12.0%	27.2%
Annual Growth Rate of Per Capita Resident Consumption	3.0%	10.7%

Note: All growth rates are based on comparable prices except otherwise noted.

Source: *China Statistical Yearbook 1992*, pp. 18–23, 164; *China Statistical Yearbook 1996*, pp. 22–29.

Table A2.7 Major Objectives of the Ninth Five-Year Plan (1996–2000)

Objectives	Basic Targets	Related Targets
Annual Growth Rate of GDP	8.09%	Per capita GNP to be quadrupled over the 1980 level
Annual Growth Rate of Per Capita Income	5% for real per capital income spent on living expenses for urban dwellers	Inflation rate to be lower than annual GNP growth rate; M1 to grow 18% annually
Annual Population Growth	1.084%	Population to be maintained under 1.3 billion
Economic System	Initially establish a socialist market economy, which is unified, open, competitive and integrated in an orderly way	The market will play a fundamental role in resource allocation under state macro-control; modern enterprise system will be established in the majority of SOEs
Industrial Structure	• Strengthen agriculture • Develop infrastructure and basic industries to make them a less restraining factor in economic growth • Develop pillar industries to lead the overall economic growth and structural upgrading • Develop high-tech industries	• The pillar industries are machinery, electronics, petrochemical, auto-making and construction • Total investment in fixed capital will be Rmb 13,000 billion, around 30% of GDP (the state-owned units will have Rmb 8,800 billion)

Table A2.7 Continued

Objectives	Basic Targets	Related Targets
Science, Culture and Social Insurance	• Promote commercialization of new technologies while strengthening basic scientific research • Technological level in key sectors to reach the world's advanced level in the late 1980s • Develop health care system, social insurance and education	• Make nine–year compulsory education universal and vocational schools to cover 60% of high schools students; • Cover 80% of urban residents and 30% of rural labour with social insurance • Cover entire population with primary health care
Efficiency	Shift growth mode, enhance overall quality and efficiency of national economy	• Energy consumption per Rmb 10,000 of GNP to drop from 2.2 tons in 1995 to 1.7 tons in 2000 (in 1995 prices) • Overall labour productivity to grow 6.5% annually
Regional Development	• Promote inter-region division of labour and avoid overlapping of regional industrial structure • Foster seven economic zones based on existing industrial locations and transportation trunk lines • Gradually reduce inter-regional development gaps	• Give priority to resource-development and infrastructure projects in central and west China • Improve terms of trade for central and west China by adjusting prices of resource-related products • Implement inter-regional fiscal transfer through the central government • Guide more foreign investors to the hinterland

Source: Xinhua News Agency, 20 March 1996.

Bibliography

BOOKS AND ARTICLES

APEC, Committee on Trade and Investment (1995), *Milestones in APEC Liberalisation: a Map of Market Opening Measures by APEC Economies*, Singapore: APEC Secretariat.

APEC, Committee for Trade and Industry (1994), *Guide to the Investment Regimes of the APEC Member Economies*, Singapore: APEC Secretariat.

Beijing University, Department of Law (ed.) (1989), *Reform and Legal Construction*, Beijing: Guangming Daily Press.

Blejer, M.I. and G. Szapary (1990), 'The Changing Role of Macroeconomic Policies in China', *Financial Development*, **27** (2), 32–35.

Bornstein, Morris (1989), 'The Soviet Centrally Planned Economy', in Bornstein, M. ed., *Comparative Economic Systems: Models and Cases*, Homewood, USA: Irwin, 295–326.

Brudvig, Lee A. (1994), 'Tax and Fiscal Reform in China and Guangdong', *East Asian Executive Reports*, **16** (4), 7–10.

Chan, Edward (1994), 'China: Reforms Foster A Growing Economy', *Institutional Investor*, **28** (12).

Chen, Albert H.Y. (1992), *Legal System of the People's Republic of China*, Singapore, Malaysia and Hong Kong: Butterworths.

Chen, K. (1991), 'The Failure of Recentralization in China: Interplay among Enterprises, Local Governments, and the Centre', in A. Hillman ed., *Markets and Politicians: Politicized Economic Choice*, Boston: Kluwer Academic Publishers.

China Industrial Economic Association (1991), *中国工业大事记* [Chronicle of China's Industrial Development], Beijing: People's Press.

Chow, Gregory C. (1993), 'Capital Formation and Economic Growth in China', *The Quarterly Journal of Economics*, August, 811-842.

Donnithorne, Audrey (1972), 'China's Cellular Economy: Some Economic Trends since the Cultural Revolution', *China Quarterly*, **52**, 605-612.

Du Xichuan and Zhang Lingyuan (1990), *China's Legal System: A General Survey*, Beijing: New World Press.

Epstein, Gene (1994), 'No–Fault Capitalism Plagues Chinese Economy', *Barron's*, **74** (3): 53–54.

Fischer. H.H. (1993), 'Joint Venturing in China: a Negotiating Experience', *East Asian Executive Reports*, May 1993, 9–16.

Fornalczyk, A. (1992), 'Competition Policy During Transition of a Centrally Planned Economy', *Fordham Corporate Law Institute*, **397**.

Gan Yuanzhi (1995), '中国商业银行改革事关全局' [China's Commercial Bank Reform is Crucial to the Whole Nation], *新世纪* [New Century Newsweek], **80,** 3–8.

Gao, Chen (1995), 'Arguments Rage Over China's Ailing Firms', *Straits Times*, Singapore, 23 October 1995, 39.

Gao Shangquan (ed.) (1994), *1994最新中国投资指南* [The 1994 Investment Guide for China], Beijing: China Economy Press.

Gregory, Paul and R. Stuart (1992), *Comparative Economic Systems,* Boston and Toronto: Houghton Mifflin Company.

Guo, S.P. and Chen, H.B. (1995), '深圳经济特区与其他经济特区发展状况的比较研究' [A Comparative Study on the Development of Shenzhen and Other SEZs], *特区经济* [SEZ Economy], Shenzhen, February 1995.

Hamlin, Kevin (1994), 'China's Rogue Banks', *International Business,* **7** (1), 32–35.

Harding, Harry (1987), *China's Second Revolution: Reform after Mao*, Washington, DC: The Brookings Institution.

Heilmann, Sebastian (1995), 'China's Efforts at Political Modernization', *Business Times* (*Trends* section), Singapore, 26–27 August 1995, iv.

Howson, N.C. (1995), 'When the Centre Doesn't Hold', *Chinese Business Review*, January–February 1995, 8–12.

Huang Xiqiang ed. (1994), *投资中国税务指南* [Tax Guide to Investors in China], Hong Kong: Shangwu Press.

Jia, Liqun and Clem Tisdell (1996), 'Resource Redistribution and Regional Income Inequality in China', *Asian Economies,* June, 48–72.

Kaye, Lincoln (1992), 'Banking in Asia: China – Bringing Up the Rear–Fast', *Far Eastern Economic Review* , **155** (38), 60–62.

Keller, P. (1989), 'Legislation in the People's Republic of China', *University of British Columbia Law Review*, **23** (3), 653.

Kornai, Janos (1980), *Economics of Shortage*, Amsterdam: North–Holland Publishing Company.

Kornai, Janos (1986), 'The Hungarian Reform Process: Visions, Hopes, and Reality', *Journal of Economic Literature,* **24** (4), 1687–1737.

Kornai, Janos (1992), 'The Post-socialist Transition and the State: Reflections in the Light of Hungarian Fiscal Problems', *American Economic Review*, **82** (2), 1–21.

Lee, Keun (1993), 'Property rights and the Agency Problem in China's Enterprise Reform', *Cambridge Journal of Economics*, **17** (2), 179–194.

Lin, Jiang (1994), 'Development of China-Funded Companies in Hong Kong', in Liu Pei Qiong ed., *Trends of China's Economy,* Hong Kong: Shangwu Press, 232–235.

Lin, Justin Y., Fang Cai, and Zhou Li (1996), *The China Miracle: Development Strategy and Economic Reform,* Hong Kong: The Chinese University Press.

Liu K. and Zhang F. (1996), '银行利率会下降吗?' [Will Banks' Interest Rates Go Lower?], *新世纪* [New Century Newsweek], Hainan, **85,** 12–14.

Liu S. and Wu Q. (eds) (1986), *China's Socialist Economy: An Outline History (1949–1984),* Beijing: Beijing Review.

Liu Xiangdong et al. (eds) (1992), *中国对外经济贸易政策指南* [Guidebook on China's Foreign Trade and Investment Policies], Beijing: Economic Management.

Lu, Ding (1994a), *Entrepreneurship in Suppressed Markets: Private-Sector Experience in China,* New York and London: Garland Publishing, Inc.

Lu, Ding (1994b), 'Regulatory Framework Against Unfair Competition for an Emerging Market Economy', *Singapore Economic Review,* **39** (1), 33–58.

Lu, J. (1994), '经济特区迈入新时代' [SEZs Entering A New Era], in *编译参考* [Compiled and Translated References], Beijing, **11**.

Ma Hong and Fang Weizhong (eds) (1993), *中国经济开发现在与未来* [Perspectives and Prospects of China's Economic Development], Beijing: Economic Management Publishing House.

Ma, Jun (1995), 'China: Central Government Credibility and Economic Overheating', *Economic Systems,* **19** (3), 237–261.

Montias, J.M. (1959), 'Planning with Material Balances in Soviet–Type Economies', *American Economic Review,* **49**, 963–985.

Nathan, A.J. (1985), *Chinese Democracy*, New York: Alfred A Knopf.

Naughton, Barry (1994), 'Chinese Institutional Innovation and Privatization From Below', *American Economic Review*, **84** (2), 266–270.

Niu, G.Y. (1993), '中国对外开放政策的发展与经济改革开放试验区的设置' [The Development of China's Open Door Policy and Setting Up of The Open Zones] in *中国黄金海岸年鉴 1993* [Yearbook of China's Golden Coast 1993], Beijing, China Tourism Publishing House.

Peebles, Gavin (1991a), *A Short History of Socialist Money*, Sydney: Allen & Unwin.

Peebles, Gavin (1991b), *Money in the People's Republic of China: A Comparative Perspective*, Sydney: Allen & Unwin.

Peng Zhiqiang and Zheng Qianggao (1993). *当代中国市场经济大全* [Encyclopaedia of the Market Economy in Contemporary China], Beijing: Business Management Press.

People's Bank of China (1994), *China's Monetary Policy in the 1990s* (in Chinese), Beijing: The Chinese Economic Press.

People's Daily and China Industrial Economic Association (1991), *中华人民共和国工业大事记* [Chronicle of Industrial Development in the People's Republic of China], Changsha: Hunan Press.

PRC Customs (1994), *中华人民共和国海关关税–政策法规实务税则* [PRC Customs Duties–Policies, Regulations, Practice and Laws], Beijing: Economic Management Press.

Qian, Yingyi (1994), 'A Theory of Shortage in Socialist Economies Based on the Soft Budget Constraint', *American Economic Review,* **84** (1), 145–156.

Qiao, Gangliang (1994), 'New Banking Opportunities for Foreign Financial Institutions in China', *Bankers Magazine*, **177** (5), 49–52.

Shapiro, J.E. et al. (1991), *Direct Investment and Joint Ventures in China,* New York: Quorum Books.

Shirk, Susan (1992), 'The Chinese Political System and the Political Strategy of Economic Reform', in Lieberthal, K. and D. Lampton eds., *Bureaucracy, Politics, and Decision Making in Post-Mao China*, Berkeley, California: University of California Press.

Sinclair–Loutit, Abbie (1992), 'Shantou to Zhuhai: The S–Z of SEZs', *Asia Money & Finance,* **7**, S27–S30.

Sino–US Information Inc. (1995), *Sino–US Europe Trading Almanac 1995,* Shanghai: Jiaotong University Press.

State Commission of Structural Reform (SCSR) (1996), 'Analysis For Enterprises Capital In The Macroeconomic Structural Changes' (in Chinese), *经济研究* [Economic Research Journal], January issue.

State Taxation Bureau (1994, 1995, 1996), *中国工商税收基本法规* [Major Laws and Regulations on Industrial and Commercial Taxation], Beijing: China Taxation Press.

State Taxation Bureau and Ministry of Finance (1991), *The Foreign-Related Tax Laws and Regulations of the People's Republic of China,* Netherlands: International Bureau of Fiscal Document.

State Taxation Bureau and Ministry of Finance (1993), *Taxation and Investment in the People's Republic of China,* Netherlands: International Bureau of Fiscal Document.

Tang, Zhimin and Ding Lu (1996), 'China's Region-Oriented Preferential Policies at the Crossroads', *Asia-Pacific Development Journal,* **3** (2), 105–124.

Walder, Andrew G. (1992), 'Local Bargaining Relationships and Urban Industrial Finance', in Lieberthal, K. and D. Lampton eds., *Bureaucracy, Politics, and Decision Making in Post-Mao China*, Berkeley, California: University of California Press.

Wang Xiyi (ed.) (1991), *An Outline of the PRC Financial System* (in Chinese), Beijing: China Finance Press.

Wang Yaotian (1994), 'China's Re-entry into the GATT', in Liu Pei Qiong (ed.), *中国大趋势* [Trends in China's Economy], Hong Kong: Shangwu Press, 200–205.

Weinstein, Bernard L. (1996), 'Development of China's Hinterland: From Autarky to Anarchy? *Challenge,* March–April, 55–59.

Wong, Christine P.W. (1991), 'Central–Local Relations in an Era of Fiscal Decline: the Paradox of Fiscal Decentralisation in Post-Mao China', *The China Quarterly*, **128**, 691–715.

Wong, John and Chen K. (1995), 'The Evolving Role of Government in China's Transitional Economy', *Journal of Far Eastern Business,* **1** (3), 113–131.

Wong, John, Rong Ma, and Mu Yang (eds) (1995), *China's Rural Enterprises: Ten Case Studies,* Singapore: Times Academic Press.

Wong, Yue-Chim Richard (1995), 'China's Economic Reform: The Next Step', *Contemporary Economic Policy*, **13** (1), 18–27.

World Bank (1984), *China: Long-Term Issues and Options*, Washington DC: World Bank.

World Bank (1988), *China: External Trade & Capital*, Washington DC: World Bank.

World Bank (1990), *China: Financial Sector Policies and Institutional Development,* New York: Oxford University Press.

World Bank (1991), *World Development Report 1991: The Challenge of Development,* New York: Oxford University Press.

World Bank (1992), *China: Reform and the Role of the Plan in the 1990s,* Washington DC: World Bank.

World Bank (1996), *World Development Report 1996: From Plan to Market,* New York: Oxford University Press.

Wu, W.M. (1990), *China's Shenzhen Special Economic Zone – A Social Benefit-Cost Analysis,* Michigan: UMI Dissertation Information Service.

Xie, Ping et al. (1992), *China's Financial Deepening and Financial Reforms* (in Chinese), Tianjing: Tianjing People's Press.

Xie, Ping (1994), *Financial Services in China,* Discussion Papers, the UN Conference on Trade and Development, **94**.

Xu Yongxian and Yu Gongbin (eds) (1994), *中国新税制指导* [Guide to New Taxation System in China], Changchun: Changchun Press.

Xu, Y.P. (1993), '我国沿边城市开放区的可喜进展' [The Favourable Development of China's Border Open Cities], in *中国经济特区与沿海经济开发区年鉴 1993* [Yearbook of China's SEZs and ETDZs 1993], Beijing: Gai Ge Press.

Yi, Gang (1994), *Money, Banking and Financial Markets in China,* Boulder and Oxford: Westview Press Inc.

Young, Ian (1993), 'Special Economic Zones: China Opens Up', *Chemical Week*, August 25/September 1, S30–S32.

Yu, K.Y. (1995), 'Beijing Rakes it in with Revamped Tax System', *Straits Times,* Singapore, 23 March.

Yu, Qiao and Xie, Ping (1996), 'Control Over Money Aggregates: Problems And Prospects in China's Transitional Economy', *WCCS Papers,* **6** (6), May.

Zhang Lianshun and Wu Fang (eds) (1994), *新税法实用指南* [A Practical Guide to New Tax Laws], Beijing: China Development Publishing House.

Zhang Xiuzhong (ed.) (1995), *新编避税与反避税实务全书* [Complete Guide to Tax Evasion and Anti-Evasion], Beijing: Chinese Economy Press.

Zhao Dexin (ed.) (1989), *中华人民共和国经济史 1967–1984* [Economic History of the PRC 1967–1984], Zhengzhou: Henan People's Press.

Zhou, Huizhong (1993), 'Bargaining and Market Decisions of State Enterprises in a Transition Economy', *China Economic Review*, **4** (1), 55–64.

Zhu Yuanliang (1993), 'China's Credit Fund Management: Problems, Features, and Solutions' (in Chinese), *中国金融* [China Finance], July.

MAIN STATISTICAL SOURCES

China Economic Yearbook Editorial Board (various years), *中国经济统计年鉴* [Almanac of China's Economy], Beijing: Economic Management Press.

China Finance Society (various years), *中国金融年鉴* [Almanac of China's Finance and Banking], Beijing: Chinese Financial Economic Press.

Ministry of Finance (various years), *中国财政年鉴* [Yearbook of China's Public Finance 1994], Beijing: China Fiscal Press 1994.

Ministry of Foreign Trade and Economic Cooperation (various years), *Almanac of China's Foreign Economic Relations,* Beijing: Foreign Trade and Economic Cooperation Press.

State Statistics Bureau (various years), *China Statistical Yearbook,* Beijing: China Statistics Press.

Xiamen Statistics Bureau (1994), *沿海开放城市,经济特区和计划单列市统计资料汇编* [Statistics on Coastal Open Cities, SEZs and Cities Under Direct Supervision of the State Council], Xiamen: Xiamen People's Press.

Index